Blue Prism
MasterClass

Developer & Professional Developer

Blue Prism
MasterClass

Developer & Professional Developer

Prasanna Kumar Ballepalli

Blue Prism MasterClass. Developer & Professional Developer
© Prasanna Kumar Ballepalli

Published by **Prasanna Kumar Ballepalli**,
H.No: 7/122, Santhamaguluru,
Prakasam District, Andhra Pradesh – 523302, India.

Printed and bound by **Kindle direct publishing (Amazon.com)**,
Brigade Gateway, 8th floor, 26/1, Dr. Rajkumar Road,
Malleshwaram(W), Bangalore-560055, Karnataka, India.

This edition published in: 2019

ISBN: 978-93-5391-769-2
Copyright © Prasanna Kumar Ballepalli 2019

INDEX

ABOUT THE AUTHOR..7

DEDICATION..9

   ACKNOWLEDGMENTS...9

ABOUT THIS BOOK...11

   ABOUT BLUE PRISM EXAM...11

CHAPTER 1. BLUE PRISM..13

CHAPTER 2. BLUE PRISM COMPONENTS.........................15

   2.1   PROCESS STUDIO...15

   2.2   OBJECT STUDIO...18

   2.3   APPLICATION MODELLER.....................................23

   2.4   CONTROL ROOM..30

   2.5   SYSTEM MANAGER..33

CHAPTER 3. NATIVE FUNCTIONS.....................................35

CHAPTER 4. DATE FUNCTIONS...39

CHAPTER 5. DATA TYPES..43

CHAPTER 6. ENVIRONMENT AND SESSION VARIABLES........45

CHAPTER 7. EXCEPTION HANDLING...............................49

CHAPTER 8. WORK QUEUES..53

CHAPTER 9. SURFACE AUTOMATION.............................55

CHAPTER 10. DELIVERY METHODOLOGY......................57

APPENDIX 1. DEVELOPER EXAM MOCK QUESTIONS...59

APPENDIX 2. PROFESSIONAL DEVELOPER EXAM MOCK QUESTIONS.......159

APPENDIX 3. DEVELOPER EXAM ANSWERS 191

APPENDIX 4. PROFESSIONAL DEVELOPER ANSWERS.....................................279

ABOUT THE AUTHOR

Prasanna Kumar, MCP (Microsoft Certified Professional), BPCA (Blue Prism Certified Architect), Six sigma certified professional, is a full-time enterprise architect, speaker, consultant, and trainer with years of industry experience. He holds computer science degree from Andhra University. For the past several years he has worked in lead qualification, Artificial Intelligence, Robotic Process Automation and .Net. He is part of successful digital transformation of companies with the aim of reducing costs, increasing revenue, and managing risks.

DEDICATION

The content of this book would not have been possible without the unyielding support of my family, friends and colleagues. I'd like to dedicate this work to my mother who is the source of my inspiration.

ACKNOWLEDGMENTS

I would like to take this opportunity to thank all of you people who made this project possible and a smooth ride. It's your support that kept me on track and the constant feedback given improved the quality of my work.

I would also like to express my special gratitude to team of "Corporativo de Digitalización, Automatización y Robótica (C.R.E.A.D), PROSEGUR" who supported me throughout the journey. Special mention is necessary for the constant encouragement that I received from the director of CREAD, Fernando Cisneros Villa, and RPA Leads team. Words are less to express my gratitude and thanks all once again.

ABOUT THIS BOOK

This book offers you tools, techniques, tips, and other information to assist you in passing the Blue Prism developer and professional certification examinations and becoming Blue Prism certified. The emphasis is on reconciling your approach to the exam with Blue Prism's viewpoint and perspective on the examination. This book is not a guide to learning development but rather a specific study tool aimed at certification exams.

This book prepares you to pass the Blue Prism certifications examination by highlighting important Blue Prism topics, providing insight into proven test-taking strategies, emphasizing key information you can expect to see on the examination, and providing exam practice questions. You have many opportunities to apply your knowledge through practice examinations and test questions. This book provides explanation of exam syllabus as well as practice questions. If you miss questions, work your way through the section again, focusing on the concepts that you missed. Similarly, you can test your knowledge and evaluate your level of preparation for the Blue Prism certification examination by taking the practice exam. After you've worked your way through this book, take the practice exam. Evaluate your results and then reread the chapters of this book related to any areas of the practice questions where you were less certain or did not select the correct answer.

ABOUT BLUE PRISM EXAM

There are no prescribed guidelines for a course of study because the examination is objective in scope and intended to test your knowledge of the Blue Prism development.

The Blue Prism developer certification examination consists of 60 four-option, multiple-choice questions. According to the Blue Prism, "The passing score for examination is 70% of total questions i.e. 42".

Developer Exam Scope

- Exception Handling
- Work Queues Management
- Development Best Practices
- Lifecycle Orientation
- Process and Object Layer
- Environment Variables, Session Variables, Credential Manger and Locks

The Blue Prism professional developer certification examination consists of 50 four-option, multiple-choice questions. According to the Blue Prism, "The passing score for examination is 70% of total questions i.e. 35".

Professional developer exam scope

- Advanced exception handling and work queues
- Advanced work queue configuration
- Development best practice
- Web services
- Browser automation
- Mainframe automation
- Java automation
- Interfacing with PDF documents
- Credentials Management and Login Agent
- Surface Automation

1

BLUE PRISM

Robotic Process Automation is field where software robots mimic the user actions to complete business processes. It is used to handle high volume, repeatable tasks generally done by the human beings in large organizations.

Robotic automation enables business operations to be agile and cost effective through rapid automation of manual, rules based, back office administrative processes, reducing cost and improving accuracy in auditing. Software robots are easy to train, and they integrate seamlessly into any system.

Some of the many benefits of RPA are:

- Cost savings
- Improved productivity
- Process improvements
- Improved quality
- Improved customer service
- Improved compliance

Blue Prism is a well-established RPA product in the market. Blue Prism robots run unattended processes remotely at an enterprise scale thus are not in the business of enabling individuals on their desktop.

Development Experience

Blue prism provides a graphical user interface for developing robots. People with no programming language can develop the robots with couple of days.

training. Blue prism provides various methods to connect to third party applications connecting as services or using code blocks.

Process Design & readability

Blue Prism uses objects to interact with applications. Blue Prisms object model means any change that you make to a business object action will take effect immediately for any process that calls it. Process studio is used to make the decisions and call the actions of business object. Blue Prism gives a far superior aesthetic feel to a built process, and its process studio is organised based on type of objects.

Blue Prism has native handlers for windows applications, Java applications, Mainframe applications and Browser Applications.

Blue Prism is designed in client server model. Blue Prism client can connect to local data base directly or to Blue Prism server. A connection should be specified at the time of login into blue prism. User Name and password should be specified if blue prism connects to local database.

2

BLUE PRISM COMPONENTS

2.1 PROCESS STUDIO

Process Studio looks like MS Visio and uses standard flow diagram symbols and notation. Process Studio is used to create, edit and test processes. Processes should be published to run from control room. Sub processes that are not required to be run from control room, are not required to be published.

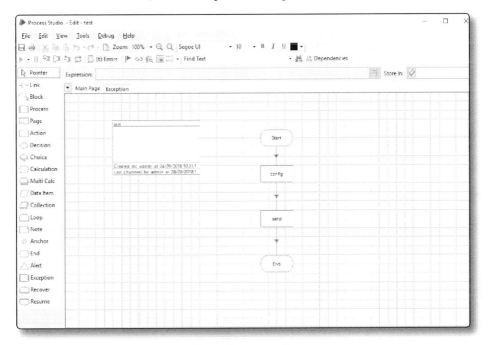

Figure: Process studio

Process Studio has below drawing tools:

▼ **Pointer**

Pointer allows objects to be highlighted and moved on the canvas.

▼ **Zoom**

Zoom implements a zoom feature, where left clicking on the process will zoom in and right clicking zooms out.

▼ **Action**

Action stage places an action on the process. Right click and select properties, to define which action library is to be used and which function within that library is specifically required. Using action stage pages from business objects will be called.

▼ **Decision**

A decision stage is used to determine the process flow within a given process. A decision can only have a True / False answer and requires one link to be drawn in and two links to be drawn out. To specify what constitutes the decision, go to the properties sheet for the decision stage and specify a comparison method and two variables, or constants to compare.

▼ **Link**

A link chains together the various stages within the flowchart and can be quickly reversed using the switch option. Most objects can have many links in, but one link out, except for data, which has no link capability, Anchor, which can have many links in and Decision, which has two links out.

▼ **Calculation**

A calculation will manipulate the data within the current process, before placing the result into a pre-determined data box. Calculation stage will be used to perform all arithmetic actions.

▼ **Anchor**

An anchor stage is a visual stage and allows links to be placed at right angles around the process, preventing the process from becoming difficult to lay out on the page. Anchor stage has neutral effect on the process flow. Misplaced anchor stage will not cause exception.

▼ Data Item

A data box contains the outputs from a given action stage and serves as a container of information which can be used in decisions and actions. Data stage is used to store the information on the page. Visibility of the data is selected in the properties of data stage. Exposure property of data item is used to make the data item an environmental variable, session variable or statistic variable.

"Hide from other pages in the process" property should be checked to restrict the visibility of the data item to the page defined.

"Reset to initial value whenever this page runs" property should be checked to reset the value of the data item on execution of the page.

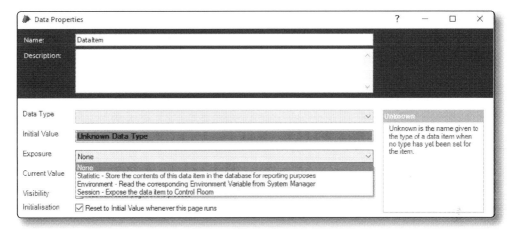

Figure: Data Item Properties

▼ Collection

A collection is a special type of data that can hold more than one item of data at any one time. Blue prism collection is equivalent to data table in c#. Collection manipulation utility can be used to perform actions on collections. Collection data type is used where it's necessary to hold multiple rows of the data.

▼ Loop Start

A Loop Start stage marks the beginning of a loop. A loop is usually used to iterate over a collection. Several actions contained within the loop are performed on each item in the collection in turn. This stage is equivalent to foreach loop in c#.

▼ **Loop End**

A Loop End stage marks the end of the loop. The process running must reach this point before the next run of the loop will be started.

▼ **Note**

A note contains information about a flowchart or element and displays the text stored in the narrative, not the name. By default, a single note is drawn onto the flowchart with the name and description given when the process was first created. The value of the note is saved in the database as log.

▼ **Start**

All flowcharts must have a Start point from which the first link flows.

▼ **End Stage**

All flowcharts must have at least one End point into which the final link(s) terminate.

▼ **Choice Stage**

Choice stage provides better way of defining multiple paths of execution based on result of expressions configured in it.

▼ **Page stage**

Page stage used to refer other pages from same object or process. It is easier to quickly understand what a process does just by looking at the Main Page, if process is divided into pages.

▼ **Alert**

Alert stage is used to send a specified message to users in process execution flow.

2.2 OBJECT STUDIO

A visual business object is used for interacting with a legacy windows application with no API. Applications which do provide an API may well be more suitably automated using a COM business object. A business object should be named with application name and screen of the application.

Objects = APP NAME + SCREEN NAME

Only published pages are visible in process studio. This is achieved via a context menu option on the page header. Once published, pages can be called from an action stage, as normal.

Having multiple objects within the object layer provides a more efficient and scalable design because:

▶ More developers can work concurrently
▶ A running process consumes only the actions it requires
▶ Application modeller is smaller and less prone to latent error
▶ Whenever a change is made within the object layer the effect on and risk to the process layer is minimised

Object Studio has the following stages those **are not available in process studio**.

▶ **Read:** Read stage is used to read data from target application's elements

▶ **Write:** Write stage is used to write the data to the target application

▶ **Navigate:** Navigate stage opens menus, clicks buttons etc.

▶ **Code:** Code stages allow advanced users to make use of .NET functionalities

▶ **Wait :** The wait stage allows you to pause a business object's execution until a certain condition has been met in the target application. Examples include waiting until a window is present or waiting for a status bar message

A wait stage has two main uses:

▶ Detecting readiness for interaction
▶ Detecting the outcome of an action

A wait stage can be used to ensure the readiness of the target application. For example, after launching the application it may be necessary to wait for it to finish loading. This could be achieved by waiting for the main application window to become visible.

Wait stage at start of each action will confirm the process is on the correct path and absorb system latency to increase the resilience of the process. Exception should be thrown on time out.

Arbitrary waits should only be used if a screen change cannot be waited for and there is no mechanism to identify the behaviour of the application.

Wait stage is unique to the object studio, not available in process studio.

Object studio Debug Toolbar

Figure: Object studio debug toolbar

- ▶ **Play** runs the process from the current point forward to the end of the current page. Speed of the execution can be controlled.

- ▶ **Step** executes the current stage by one step. If the next stage lies inside another page, process or business object then the execution control navigates to that position.

- ▶ **Step over** behaves like the "Step" command, except that if the current stage is a page reference stage or a subprocess then all stages contained inside the referenced page/process are executed in one go, and the flow jumps to the next stage on the current page. In this sense, the flow has not stepped "into" the nested sub-page but stepped "over" it.

- ▶ **Step out** control continues running until the flow moves out of the current page/sub-process back to the stage which called the current page/sub-process.

- ▶ **Pause** pauses the execution at its current point. Play, step, step out or step over should be used to resume the execution.

- ▶ **Reset** restarts the debugger. Reset button should be clicked before executing a new page in object studio.

- ▶ **Errors** shows the errors and warnings in current page.

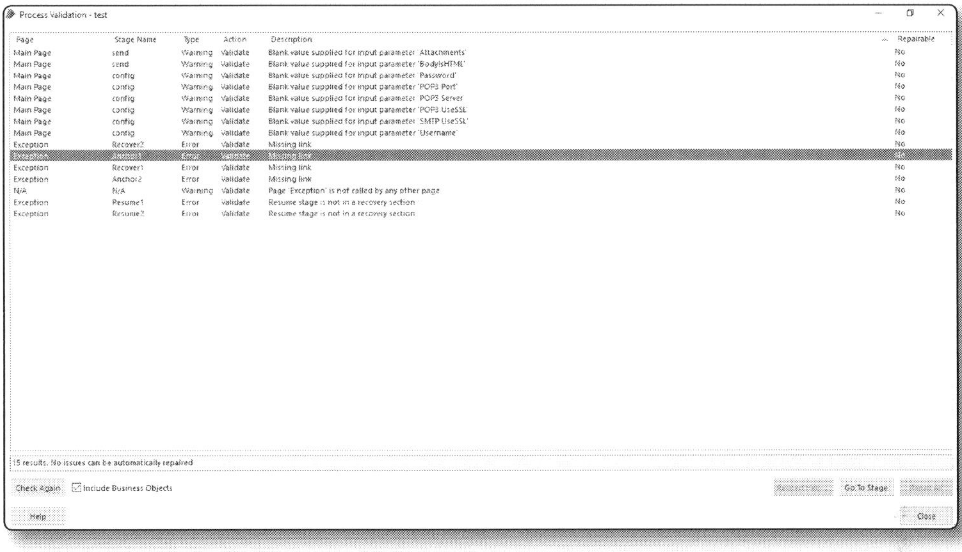

Figure: Errors in a page

- **View Break Points** lists all the break points that are in the current object or process.

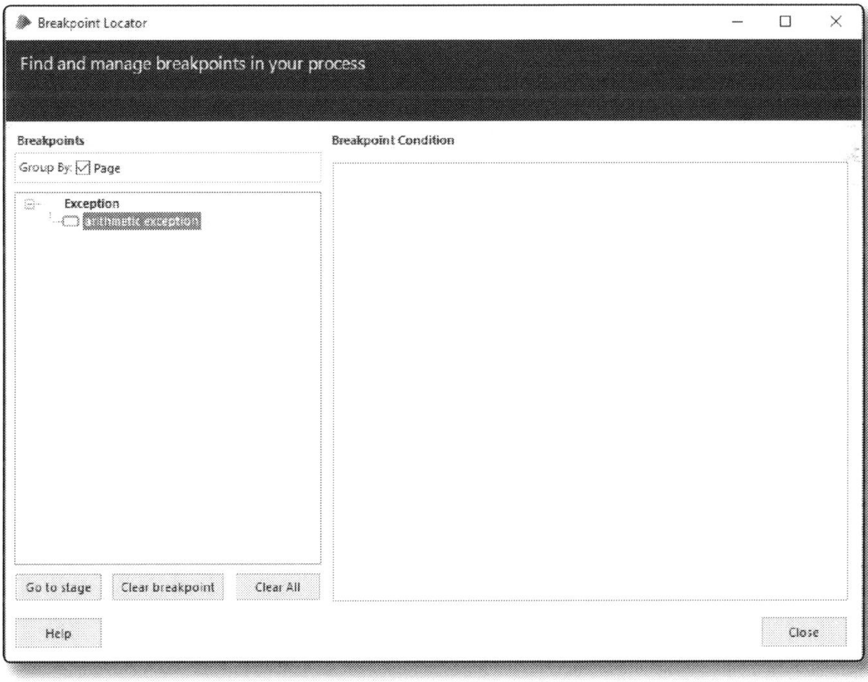

Figure: Break Points dialogue box

- **View Data Item Watches:** The data item watches window is used for monitoring the current value of data items during debug in Process Studio.

- **View Process MI:** The Process MI (Management Information) form is used to analyse previous sessions of a process. Session log data is extracted from the database.

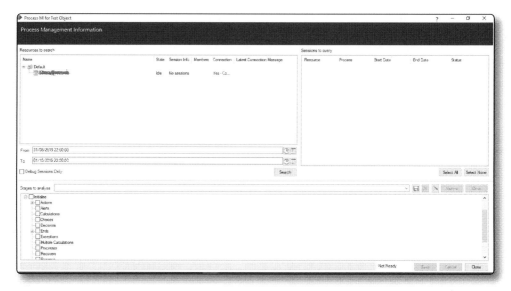

Figure: Process Management Information

▼ **Full Screen Mode** maximises the blue prism object studio.

- **Find   text:** is used to search the text in the solution.

Business Object Mode

Business object Mode is useful when Blue Prism is running as a 32-bit process and the target application is a 64-bit process, or vice versa.

▼ **Fore ground:** if the object should never have more than one instance running at the same time on the same resource, set to foreground. This business object can run at the same time as other back ground business object.

▶ **Back ground:** if the object is developed to support multiple instances running at same time, set to back ground. This business object can run at the same time as foreground business object or back ground business object.

▶ **Exclusive:** if this object should never be run at the same time as any other object, and requires exclusive access to the desktop, set to exclusive. This business object cannot run at the same time as any other business object.

2.3 APPLICATION MODELLER

{element type} – {element name} is the local naming convention of application modeller elements. For example, window – Win32 is the proper name of a window that has been spied in Win32 mode.

Application modeller is important feature of the object studio which is used to capture the target system elements in Blue Prism. Once the elements are captured using application modeller, these elements can be used in object studio stages.

In Application modeller, attributes are matched against an expression rather than a fixed value. The expression is determined by a match type, and the match types that are available.

▶ **Equal** matches the given value exactly.

▶ **Not Equal** matches only if it is anything other than the given value.

▶ **Less than** matches if it is less than the given value.

▶ **Greater than** matches if it is greater than the given value.

▶ **Less than or Equal** matches if it is less than or equal to the given value.

▶ **Greater than or Equal** matches if it is greater than or equal to the given value.

▶ **Wildcard** matches against a wildcard expression in which * represents any or no characters, matches any single character and # matches any single number.

▶ **Reg Ex** matches against a regular expression.

▼ **Range** matches if it falls within a specific range of values (inclusive). The syntax for the value must be in the form X. Y i.e. the lower (X) and upper (Y) values are separated by two dots.

▼ **Dynamic** matches an expression within Read, Write, Navigate, and Wait stages at runtime.

Application Manager mode

Application Manager mode is used to configure Blue prism to interact with applications of different bits. This can be useful, for example, if Blue Prism is running as a 32-bit process and the target application is a 64-bit process, or vice versa.

The available modes are:

▼ **Embedded (default):** This is the default mode. In this mode, Application Manager runs in the same process as Blue Prism itself.

▼ **External, 32-bit mode:** Application Manager runs in a separate process when interfacing with the target application. The Application Manager process is always 32 bits.

▼ **External, 64-bit mode:** Application Manager runs in a separate process when interfacing with the target application. The Application Manager process is always 64 bits.

▼ **External, OS address size:** Application Manager runs in a separate process when interfacing with the target application. The Application Manager process matches the operation system address size. e.g. on 64-bit Windows, it will be a 64-bit process.

▼ **External, Blue Prism address size:** Application Manager runs in a separate process when interfacing with the target application. The Application Manager process matches Blue Prism's address size. e.g. if Blue Prism is running as a 64-bit process, the Application Manager process will also be 64 bits.

Spy Modes

Application modeller user window spy tool (spy++) for spying application's elements. There are four mode of spy tool:

▼ **Win32 Mode**

Windows 32 mode will identify most of the application's elements. Win32 mode will fail to identify elements if ActiveX components are used in target application design.

▼ **Win 32 Mode Application Attributes**

- **WindowText:** The text in the window. The values will be changed as the robot navigates through page.

- **ClassName:** The name given to a type of control. In HTML elements class name is used to apply CSS (Cascading Style Sheets).

- **CtrlID:** The ID given to the element by the owning application. Most of the application's elements have this parameter empty.

- **Ordinal:** The order in which the element is created by the target application. Ordinal is used to define how application is loaded in the operating system.

- **X**: The X location, in pixel coordinates, of the element relative to the parent window.

- **Y**: The Y location, in pixel coordinates, of the element relative to the parent window.

- **Width**: The width of the spied element, in pixels.

- **Height**: The height of the spied element, in pixels.

- **Visible** indicates whether the element is visible. An element may be present. Wait stage action "Check exist" will return true even if element is hidden.

- **Enabled** indicates whether the element is available for interaction in the target application. Some elements are greyed out as per the application design flow.

- **Active** indicates whether the window is "in focus".

- **Child Count** indicates how many child windows the element contains.

HTML Mode

HTML mode is used to identify the elements of the browser applications.

Each tab of internet explorer is given a unique index based on the order in which the process for that session was created. For example, the main parent process is given the index of 0, whereas the first tab of the process is given the Child Index of 1. The Child Index parameter is specified in the attach action of a navigate stage.

If any problem is encountered that prevent from using either of the three spying modes, an alternative exists in the form of the Application Navigator.

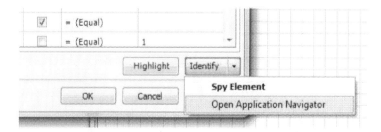

Pop-up Windows

Depending on how the web application has been built, you might need to create a separate business object to interface with a popup window. it might be best to build a separate generic object to handle IE pop-up windows.

HTML mode attributes

- ▶ **X**: The horizontal coordinate of the spied element's upper left corner, relative to its parent element.

- ▶ **Y**: The vertical coordinate of the spied element's upper left corner, relative to its parent element.

- ▶ **Width**: The width of the spied element, in screen pixels.

- ▶ **Height**: The height of the spied element, in screen pixels.

- ▶ **Path** represents the path of the element in the Document Object Model (DOM) of HTML document.

- ▶ **TagName**: The name of the tag representing element, as declared in the html document source. For example, the tag name of a button is "button" cause "<button >Submit</button>" is used to create button in HTML.

- **ClassName**: The class name of the tag representing the element, as used in cascading style sheets (CSS). For example, in the html tag <button class=”Clsbutton”>, the class name is “Clsbutton”.

- **ID**: The ID of the html tag representing the element, as specified in the html source. For example, the tag <buttton id=”button> has an id of “button”.

- **Title:** The title of the html tag representing the element.

- **Link**: The target URL of a hyperlink.

- **InputType**: The type of data to be input in the HTML element.

- **Value**: The value displayed in the element.

- **Enabled** indicates whether the element is enabled. Disabled elements are not capable of receiving keyboard or mouse input.

- **Checked** indicates whether the element is checked.

AA (Active Accessibility) Mode

Microsoft Active Accessibility is an Application Programming Interface (API) for user interface accessibility. Active Accessibility is designed to help Assistive Technology products interact with standard and custom user interface (UI) elements of an application , as well as to access, identify, and manipulate an application's UI elements.

AA mode attributes

- **Checked** indicates whether an option is selected.

- **Collapsed** indicates whether an option is collapsed, meaning that its children are hidden.

- **Expanded** is the inverse of the Collapsed attribute.

- **Focusable** indicates whether an element is focusable. If element is in focus, keyboard input will reach directly.

- **Focused** indicates whether an element is focused, which means that it receives any keyboard input.

- **Invisible** indicates whether the element is visible on the screen. Any element which is located off the screen will not be visible.

▼ **Linked** attribute value is true when the type of element is a hyperlink.

▼ **Mixed:** The state is Mixed if the toggle state is indeterminate. For example, a checkbox may begin in a state which is neither set (True) nor unset (False), indicating that the user has not yet selected an option. In this case the state is said to be indeterminate.

▼ **Movable** indicates whether the element can be moved in the application.

▼ **MultiSelectable** indicates whether more than one item in the element can be selected concurrently. Relevant only for elements such as listviews, radio boxes which allow items to be selected.

▼ **Protected** indicates whether the data contained in the element is masked from view, such as in a password field.

▼ **Read-only** represents whether the data in the element can be changed.

▼ **Selectable** indicates whether the element can be selected.

▼ **Selected** indicates whether the element is selected.

▼ **Sizable** indicates whether the element can be resized.

▼ **Unavailable** indicates whether the element is available for interaction. Elements that are invisible are unavailable to interact.

Java Mode

Java Mode in Blue Prism is used to spy the elements of java applications.

Java mode attributes

▼ **Active** indicates a window is currently the active window.

▼ **Armed** indicates that the element is armed. This is usually used on buttons that have been pressed but not yet released, and the mouse pointer is still over the button.

▼ **Busy** indicates the current element is busy. This is usually used on elements such as progress bars, sliders, or scroll bars to indicate that they are in a state of transition.

▼ **Checked** indicates this element is currently checked.

▼ **Collapsed** indicates this element is collapsed. Tree View element has collapsed attribute value set to false if all child elements are expanded.

▼ **Editable** indicates the user can change the contents of this element.

▼ **Enabled** indicates whether this element is enabled. An element that is not enabled cannot be manipulated by the user.

▼ **Expanded** indicates this element is expanded.

▼ **Focusable** indicates this element can accept keyboard focus. Being focusable means all events resulting from typing on the keyboard will normally be passed to it when it has focus.

▼ **Focused** indicates this element currently has the keyboard focus.

▼ **Horizontal** indicates the orientation of this element is horizontal, as opposed to vertical. This is relevant for elements such as scrollbars and trackbars which can appear in more than one orientation.

▼ **Iconified** indicates this element is minimized and is represented only by an icon.

▼ **Modal** Indicates something must be done with this element before the user can interact with an element in a different window. This is usually associated only with dialogs.

▼ **MultipleLine** indicates this (text) element can contain multiple lines of text.

▼ **Multiselectable** indicates this element allows more than one of its children to be selected at the same time.

▼ **Pressed** indicates this element is currently pressed.

▼ **Resizable** indicates the size of this element is not fixed.

▼ **Selectable** indicates this element is the child of an element that allows its children to be selected, and that this child is one of those children that can be selected, if desired by the user.

▼ **Selected** indicates this element is the child of an element which allows its children, to be selected.

▼ **Showing** indicates this element, the element's parent, the element's parent's parent, and so on, are all visible. Any item in the chain might be occluded by some other showing element.

▼ **SingleLine** indicates element can contain only a single line of text.

- **Transient** indicates this element is transient. Transient elements are not usually useful for automation purposes. Care should be taken to used them in wait stage.
- **Vertical** indicates that the orientation of this element is vertical, as opposed to horizontal. This is usually associated with elements such as scrollbars and trackbars which can appear in more than one orientation.
- **Visible** indicates this element is visible.

2.4 CONTROL ROOM

Published processes are run from Blue Prism called Control Room. Though processes are debugged in process studio, they should be published to run from control room or to be used in schedules. Only published process will be shown in control rom available processes part.

The machines which are connected to same Blue prism server will be shown in resources part.

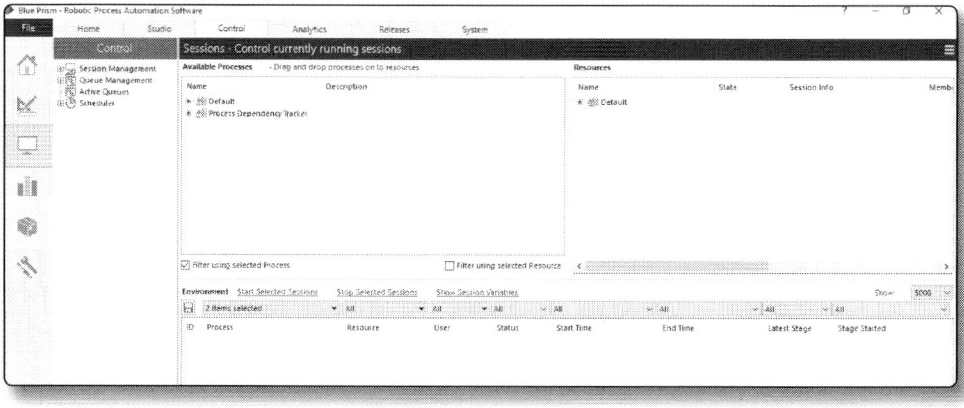

Figure: Control Room

- **Session:** A session represents a process which is currently assigned to a resource. These are the statuses of a session. Pending, Running, Completed, Terminated, Stopped.
- **Work Queue:** A queue contains several work items, which a session can lock and work within a process or business object. Working the queues is done using the work queues business object.

▼ **Active Queues:** Active queues allows to set a target number of resources which should be working the queue. Sessions will be created by Blue Prism using the active queues configuration.

▼ **Scheduler:** Scheduler is the functionality used by blue prism to automate the execution of the processes. Schedule comprises of one or more tasks whose execution is sequentially linked.

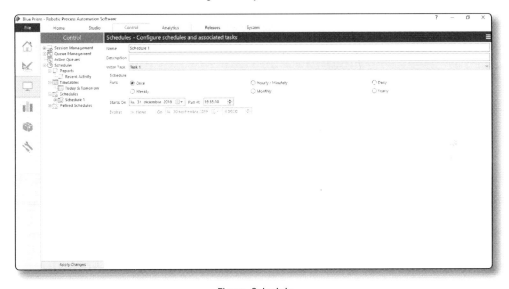

Figure: Schedule

Recent activity option of scheduler is used to reports for all schedules which ran in the time selected.

Task

Task is a set of sessions which are to be executed concurrently. Each task can contain an arbitrary number of sessions. When the task is executed, each session is first created and, once they are all registered and pending on their host resources, they are executed.

If a task is set to 'fail fast', if any session fails to be created, all sessions will be terminated, and the task will be terminated. Likewise, if any session's execution causes an error, all other sessions will be terminated, and the task will be terminated.

If a task is set to not fail fast, any session creation failures are logged but do not cause the task to fail. Equally, any individual session executions which cause an error are logged, but any other running sessions continue. Note that, if not failing fast, a task is marked as terminated only if all its sessions fail.

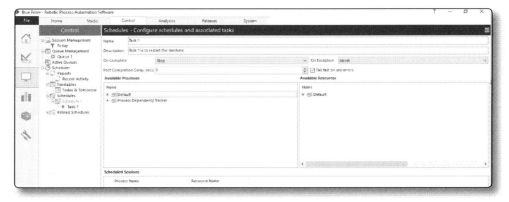

Figure: Task

Retired Schedules

A schedule will be retired to de-activate its execution and to remove it from schedule reports. A retired schedule cannot be modified unless its restored as normal schedules.

Analytics

Analytics section is used to create dashboards. Dashboards consist of a list of tiles each of which provides a visual representation of information derived from Blue prism data base. Tile provides the settings that will be used to build the data source from Blue Prism database and display it visually within the dashboard.

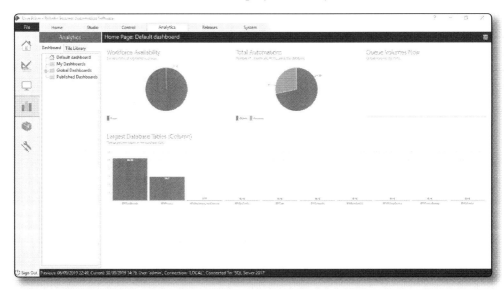

Figure: Dash Board

Releases – Packages and Releases

Release manager allows to create packages by bundling blue prism processes, objects, credentials, environment variables etc. These packages will be exported as Blue Prism releases to another environment.

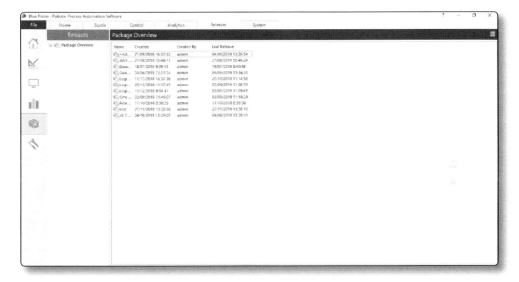

Figure: Release Manager

2.5 SYSTEM MANAGER

System Manager is where Blue Prism's own settings are kept. Below tasks will be performed in system manager.

- ▶ Create and maintain user accounts, roles and permissions.

- ▶ Retire resources, Processes and Business Objects.

- ▶ View Process or Business Object change history.

- ▶ Manage external web services & expose blue prism processes or objects as web services.

- ▶ Manage work queues, encryption of key item of queue.

- ▶ View Exception types that are defined in processes or Business objects.

- ▶ Mange environmental variables.

▼ Resource Management such as creating resource pools, retiring resource machines

▼ Work Queue Creation and configuration.

▼ Unlocking environment Locks.

▼ Configuration of Sign-on settings.

▼ Management of credentials.

▼ Configuration of Encryption Schemes.

▼ Configuration of design control.

▼ Configuration of Licenses, archiving settings,

Reporting.

3

NATIVE FUNCTIONS

"Native" in this context means that a method (function) is provided by Blue Prism, rather than being developed by user.

Navigate stage functions

▶ **Global Send Key:** This function is used to Send keys to the active application. The target application must have focus to receive the keys.

▶ **Global send key events:** This function is used to Send keys to the application using events. These events take place at the lowest level and are received by whichever application is currently focused.

Special characters should be enclosed in curly braces (e.g. {SPACE}, {ESC}, {PGUP}, {PGDN}, {LEFT}, {RIGHT}, {UP}, {DOWN}). The modifiers "<" and ">" change the following letter into a key-down or key-up operation (respectively), instead of a full key-press (i.e. key-down followed by key-up operation). For example, "<{CTRL}s>{CTRL}" simulates depressing the control key, pressing "s" and releasing the control key again. Special characters (such as "<", ">", "{", "}") should be enclosed in curly braces if meant literally.

▶ **Activate Application** activates the application, i.e. brings to the foreground.

▶ **Global Mouse Click Centre** clicks at the centre of the Active Accessibility element. the target application must have focus.

▶ **Global Mouse Click** clicks the element at the specified position, using a global mouse click. The position is relative to the top left of the element's bounding rectangle.

▼ **Get Table** is used to get the Active Accessibility table specified.

▼ **Invoke Javascript Function** calls the specified JavaScript function. This can be a standard javascript function, or one which is defined in the target HTML page.

▼ **Insert Javascript Fragment** inserts the supplied JavaScript fragment into the target document. This can be a mixture of methods and variables. The methods can later be invoked using the corresponding method.

▼ **Check Exists** check the element exists - True or False.

▼ **Document Loaded** checks if the current document has loaded - True or False. Relevant only for browser applications. This check should not be used if robot is already on the page which you are waiting to load, otherwise it is more appropriate to use Parent Document Loaded on an element on the target page. Parent Document Loaded includes an implicit Check exists on the element as well as a Document Loaded check.

▼ **Parent Document Loaded** checks the element exists and that the entire page and all its child frames are fully loaded. Parent Document Loaded includes an implicit Check exists on the element as well as a Document Loaded check.

▼ **Is Connected** checks whether the business object is currently connected to the application (be it through launching or attaching).

String Functions

▼ **Chr** return the ASCII character represented by the input numeric.

▼ **Concatenate** adds (concatenates) the input strings.

▼ **Instr(String, Search String)** returns an integer specifying the start position of the first occurrence of one string within another.

▼ **Left(String, Length)** returns a string containing a specified number of characters from the left side of a string.

▼ **Len(String)** returns an integer containing either the number of characters in a string.

▼ **Lower(String)** converts the input string into lowercase.

▼ **Mid(String, start point, Length)** returns a string that contains a specified number of characters starting from a specified position in a string.

▼ **Replace(String, pattern, new text)** returns a string in which a specified substring has been replaced with another substring a specified number of times.

▼ **Right(text, Length)** returns a string containing a specified number of characters from the Right side of a string.

▼ **Startswith(Text, StartText)** returns true if input text starts with startText.

▼ **Trim(Text)** returns the text without leading or trailing spaces.

▼ **TrimEnd(Text)** gets text that is the input with any whitespace trimmed from the end.

▼ **TrimStart(Text)** returns text that is the input with any whitespace trimmed from the start.

▼ **Upper(Text)** converts the input string into uppercase.

Number Functions

Below are some of the important number functions.

▼ **Decpad(number,decimal places)** returns text representing a number with decimal places padded out with zeros.

DecPad(10,2) returns "10.00".

▼ **Power (^)** raises a number to the power of another. For example, $10^4 = 10*10*10*10 = 10000$.

▼ **RndDn (Number, Places)** gets a number rounded down to several given decimal places.

For example, RndDn(3.55,1) returns in 3.5

▼ **RndUp (Number, Places)** gets a number rounded up to several given decimal places.

For example, RndUp(3.57,1) returns in 3.6

▼ **Round (Number, Places)** rounds a value to the nearest integer or to the specified number of fractional digits.

▼ **Sqrt(Number)** returns the square root of a specified number. For example, sqrt (9) returns 3.

4

DATE FUNCTIONS

Below intervals are used to add the time using date functions.

Interval	DateAdd	DateDiff
0	Year	Year
1	Week	Week of year *(Calendar week)*
2	(n/a)	Weekday *(Full 7-day week)*
3	(n/a)	Second
4	Quarter	Quarter
5	Month	Month
6	(n/a)	Minute
7	(n/a)	Hour
8	(n/a)	Day of year
9	(n/a)	Day

DateDiff (interval, date1, date2)

The recommended way to find the difference between two Dates, Times, or DateTimes is to subtract them.

For example, MakeDate(01;1;2000) - MakeDate(01;1;2010) will return a TimeSpan 3653.00:00:00.

Examples

To calculate the number of weeks between 01/1/2000 and 01/1/2010 use DateDiff(1; MakeDate(29;5;1968);MakeDate(26;5;1999)). This will correctly return 522.

DateAdd(interval, number,date)

The Blue prism recommended way to add an interval to a Date, Time, or DateTime is to add a TimeSpan.

Example, *MakeDate(26,5,1999) + MakeTimeSpan(3, 0, 0, 0)* would result in 29/05/1999.

For times, *MakeTime(12,30,0) + MakeTimeSpan(0, 1, 5, 3)* would result in 13:35:03.

FormatDate (Date, DateFormat)

This function is used to format a date into a desired form, or to extract a smaller piece of information (such as the day of the week) from a full date.

Examples

FormatDate("02-11-2016", "D") will return "02 November 2016"

FormatDate("02 Nov 2016","d") will return "2/11/2016"

FormatDate("02-11-2016", "M") will return "2 November"

FormatDate("02-11-2016", "dddd") will return "Wednesday"

FormatDate("02/11/2016", "yyyy-MM-dd") will return "2016-11-02"

FormatDate("02/11/2016", "MMM dd, yyyy") will return "Nov 02, 2016"

FormatDateTime (Date, DateFormat)

This function is used to format a datetime into a desired form, or to extract a smaller piece of information (such as the day of the week) from a full datetime.

Parameters

The two parameters are as follows:

▼ **Date**

The datetime value to be formatted as a text value.

▼ **Format**

The format string, which specifies the form of the desired output. This can either be inputted as a single letter denoting a standard datetime format or a string denoting a custom datetime format.

Examples

FormatDate("02-11-2016 09:23:43", "t") will return "09:23"

FormatDate("02 Nov 2016 09:23:43","F") will return "02 November 2016 09:23:43"

FormatDate("02-11-2016 21:23:43", "h:m tt") will return "9:23 PM"

FormatDate("02-11-2016 21:23:43", "dd/MM/yy HH:m:s") will return "02/11/16 21:23:43"

MakeDate (Day, Month, Year)

MakeDate() is used to create a date from numbers.

For example

MakeDate(21,6,2005) will return the date 21st June 2005

MakeDate(21,6,1995) will return the date 21st June 1995

MakeDate(5,12,29) will return the date 5th December 2029

MakeDate(5,12,30) will return the date 5th December 1930

AddDays (date, numDays)

This function will add a certain number of days to a chosen date.

AddDays("01/01/2006", 10) will return the date "11/01/2006".

AddMonths (date, numMonths)

This function will add a certain number of months to a chosen date.

AddMonths("01/01/2006", 10) will return the date "01/11/2006".

Now ()

This function will return the current date and time and date as a datetime data item.

Today ()

This function will return the current date as a date data item.

5

DATA TYPES

Blue Prism has the following data items.

▶ **Text** is used to store words or phrases as well as numerical identifiers such as account numbers.

▶ **Password** is used to store passwords or any text that must always be kept secret. Blue Prism will take steps to ensure that data entered password fields is not inadvertently displayed. For example, a password will never be displayed on-screen, cannot be copied into a plain text data item, and will not be directly viewable in the XML of a saved or exported process. However, there is an obvious security risk associated with storing password values within a process and as such we do not recommend it.

▶ **Number** is used to store numerical values and currencies.

▶ **Time Span** is used to store periods of time.

▶ **Date** is used to store a date.

▶ **Date Time** is used to store a specific moment in time at a specific time in history.

▶ **Time** is used to store the time of the day.

▶ **Flag** is used to store a true or false value.

6

ENVIRONMENT AND SESSION VARIABLES

Environment variables are used to store process or application information required to work the business process that may be changed between environments (development /production).

The purpose of using environment variables is so that minor changes to the configuration of a solution can be made without the need to make development changes to the objects or processes. Changes to the environmental will reflect in the next execution of the robot. Robot needs to be rerun to get the updated value of environmental variables.

Environment Variables should be used to store configurable information such as: -

▶ Network Paths.
▶ Email.
▶ Database details.
▶ web service configuration details.
▶ System configuration such as URLs.

Environmental variables are created in System – Processes – Environment Variables.

Exposure property of the data item should be chosen as environment to make the data item as environmental variable.

Session Variables

Session variables are data items that can be modified at run time from Control Room. Any configuration that may need changing whist a process session is running will be exposed as a Session variable. A Session Variable is created by simply changing the exposure option for a data item in the Data Properties window from None to Session.

Show variable option from control room should be used to amend the session variable.

Changes to the session variable will reflect immediately in the execution of the robot.

Running processes in Control Room can now be stopped on "Request" when using the IsStopRequested function in the process.

7

EXCEPTION HANDLING

An exception is an event, which occurs during the execution of a program, that disrupts the normal flow of the program's instructions.

Exceptions occur during the running of a process for various reasons. There may be, for example:

▼ A mistake in the process itself (e.g. an invalid expression entered into a calculation).

▼ Failure to match an element (e.g. trying to 'press' a button that doesn't exist).

▼ Something wrong with the data (e.g. an account types we don't know how to work).

An exception will bubble upwards towards the main page of the parent process, ultimately bringing the process to a stop if subpages do not have exception handling implemented. Exception block on the Main Page to handle exceptions that 'bubble up'. Retry loops on work subpages – to attempt system errors again.

Business objects usually contain very little (or no) exception handling. Exception handling and retrying tends to be done on layers above the object layer. Blocks in main page generally covers used to work queue case management.

By default, a Recover stage will attract any exception occurring on its page, and this can sometimes lead to an infinite loop. A Block is a mechanism for isolating exception handling to a specific area and is a good way to prevent an infinite loop. Exceptions occurring during Recovery Mode cannot themselves be recovered.

System exception represents the application related problem.

Business exception represents the all business logic errors.

Validation Exception is thrown when the data input into the process has been validated and failed.

System Exception Try Once is same as any other system exception but marked as one that should not be retried.

Login System Exception occurs if an exception occurs attempting to log into a system.

System Unavailable Exception is thrown If a system is not available, it is a System Unavailable Exception and no work queue items should be marked with an exception.

Internal Exception is the type of exception that is generated by Blue Prism itself. Already connected to an application, Not Connected, Syntax error, Missing data etc... are the examples of the internal exceptions.

Exception reason "Automatically set exception at clean up" is set up by Blue Prism if queue case is not declared as completed or exception. This could occur when machine restarts when Process is in execution, Process gets terminated before declaring previous item or takes another case with our declaring the previous case.

The resume stage allows the process to resume normal flow of execution after recovering from and exception.

Recover Stage is where execution will jump to when an exception occurs.

Exception Stage allows the process to raise the custom exceptions and stop execution.

- ▼ The current exception is released when the 'Preserve the type and current details of the exception' checkbox is ticked.

- ▼ A new exception is generated when the 'Preserve the type and current details of the exception' checkbox is not ticked.

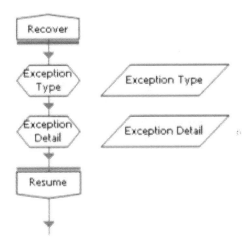

Capturing Exception Details

The advantage of capturing exception details is that the risk of another exception occurring during Recovery Mode is eliminated and any activities performed after catching the exception can be protected by a secondary piece of exception handling.

Below cases should be taken care while implementing exception handling.

▼ **Infinite Re-throw Loop:** This happens when exception handling logic throws an exception back to itself and falls into a never-ending cycle of throw-recover-throw-recover.

▼ **Infinite Retry Loop:** This happens when exception retry logic does not contain any mechanism to break out of the loop.

▼ **Nested Retries:** This happens when one sequence of retry logic sits within another and the numbers of retries in each multiply together.

▼ **Nesting Exception Handling:** Blue Prism has no concept of multiple, 'nested' Recovery Modes - Recovery Mode is either on or off. Blocks should not be nested together.

▼ **Generating another exception without resuming:** When a Recover stage is followed by an Exception stage, failure to tick the 'Preserve...' checkbox will result in a second exception.

▼ **Stepping Past the Resume Stage:**

▼ **Misleading Exception Detail:** Wrong exception details will mislead the process controller that try to analyse the logs from control room.

▼ **Missing Exception Detail:** If the properties of an Exception stage are left blank then it will generate an exception with no detail.

8

WORK QUEUES

The Work Queue feature provides this functionality to store, manage, share, and report on Process work. A work queue is an internal configurable list that enables a Process to manage its workload. A Process can use different work queues and a work queue can be shared by multiple Processes if required.

Work Queue Tags

Work Queue Tags are easily search in Queue Management and are reported on robot work report. Tags are used to get total numbers of different work.

Work queue tags are used for more control over how Work Queue items that are locked and worked in a process. Internal – Work Queues Business Object's Tag Item Action is used to tag the work queue item. Tags can be used when getting items from the Work Queue. Tags can be used to filter the items to retrieve by the presence or absence of a specific tag, by giving the appropriate arguments to the Tag Filter input parameter of the Get Next Item action.

+ filter is used to retrieve specific tag cases from work queue. - filter is used to retrieve items without a specific tag.

For example, by setting the Tag Filter to be "+Work Type1; +Customer Type2; -Work Source1" the next item with the "Work Type1" and "Customer Type2" tags and without a "Work Source1" tag will be returned.

Work Queue tags are reported on the Blue Prism Performance Report - All Exception Work Queue items should be tagged as either 'System Exception' or 'Business Exception' - Other tags are useful to get total numbers of different work or case type.

Work Queue Status

The status is a useful way of recording how far through your process a Work Queue item has been worked. If an item is to be re-worked following an exception the Status could be used to skip steps in the process flow that have already been completed for that item in the process flow.

By default, the order in which items are selected by Get Next Item is First-In-First-Out (FIFO), or in other words, the same order in which they were added to the queue. However, the order can be modified by setting the Priority parameter.

The Priority is an optional parameter to the Add to Queue action and when this parameter is not passed, the Priority is assumed to be zero. Get Next Item selects items in order of lowest Priority number first, so an item with Priority set to 1 will be selected before an item with Priority set to 2. Where items have the same Priority, the FIFO principle applies.

Active Queues

Instead of creating sessions separately in Control Room and then moving to the queue management page to see the results, active queues allow developers to set a target number of resources which should be working the queue, Blue Prism uses the active queue configuration to determine how to achieve that target. To stop a session which is running on behalf of an active queue, a 'stop request' should be made to the session.

9

SURFACE AUTOMATION

Surface automation is used if the application is not installed on same machine of Blue Prism or application is accessible only from remote access technologies.

Surface Automation is entirely dependent on the target application being clearly visible. If the application is minimized or obscured by another window, then Surface Automation techniques cannot succeed. This can be difficult to achieve whilst you are developing your objects, and good tip is to avoid maximizing either the application or Object Studio, and instead try to arrange them 'side by side'. Surface automation uses region mode to spy the elements from target application.

Region

A region is a rectangular area 'geographically' bound to a parent Win32 element. Blue Prism finds the parent element first and then focuses in on the child Region.

Regions take on some of the attributes of the parent Win32 element, and these attributes may need adjustment from the default.

Character Matching

As with data input, Surface Automation has limited options for getting data out of an application because of the paucity of information offered by a thin-client. In some situations, the clipboard can be useful, but often the only option is to analyse the image, either by OCR or by Blue Prism's own technique of Character Matching.

Character Matching ability to discern text characters from an image. In brief, the technique involves creating a template of font characters which can then be used.

to inspect a screenshot, and by finding matching patterns of pixels, characters and words can be deduced.

Font Smoothing

Font Smoothing is a Windows setting designed to make fonts easier for people to read by blurring (antialiasing) the edges of text characters. This setting disrupts Character Matching and we need it to be switched off on all Blue Prism PCs.

Read Text with OCR

Blue Prism's "Read Text with OCR" action uses Google's Tesseract open source OCR (Optical Character Recognition) engine to be able to read text without identifying the font or disabling font smoothing.

Radio Buttons and Checkboxes cannot be read as text, but a Wait stage can be used to detect their condition.

Wait stages can also be used to detect, and wait for, a difference between a design time image and it's run time equivalent. This is how Surface Automation can keep pace with the state of an application.

There are many varieties of combo box and drop-down lists, each with their own behaviour. As such there is no single method of integration and the developer must be prepared to find the ideal technique, which may be a combination of keystrokes, mouse clicks and Read stages.

A 'dynamic' region can be used to travel down a list, or a 'list region' can be used to make a repeating sequence of regions. Both require pixel level precision.

Some characters in some fonts are visually identical, and such 'character conflicts' require logical interpretation. Capital I and lower-case L are a classic example.

Image searching, and matching is achieved through pixel-by-pixel comparison, and the size of a region and its search area can impact on performance.

10

DELIVERY METHODOLOGY

Process Definition Document (PDD) defines the business process at a granular key stroke level and describes all the business rules and decisions that are made.

Functional Requirement Questionnaire (FRQ) Documents the functionality to enable the process solution to run unattended whilst meeting the demands of the business.

The Solution Design document (SDD) is a high-level design document that describes how the entire solution is going to be built. The SDD should be peer reviewed by an experienced Blue Prism developer or design control body of organization.

The Process Definition Instruction (PDI) is a low-level design document that describes exactly how the process should be built including Work Queues, Environment Variables, Alerts, etc. The PDI should be peer reviewed by an experienced Blue Prism developer or design control body of organization.

Object Design Instruction (ODI) describes in detail a single Blue Prism Business Object, including all the actions in the object and all the inputs and outputs to those actions.

Operational Impact Document (OID) describes in detail the impact on the Operation from the delivery of the automated solution.

Document	Created By
Initial Process Analysis	Blue Prism analyst or Blue Prism developer
Process Definition Document	Client SME and/or Blue Prism analyst
Functional Requirements Questionnaire	Client SME and/or Blue Prism analyst
Solution Design Document	Blue Prism developer
Operational Impact Document	Blue Prism analyst
Process Design Instruction	Blue Prism developer
Object Design Instruction	Blue Prism developer

Document creation in Blue Prism RPA Team

Appendix 1

DEVELOPER EXAM MOCK QUESTIONS

1. Which part of the Blue Prism would be used to configure business rules and logic?

    A. Application Modeller
    B. Object Studio
    C. Process Studio
    D. Control Room

2. Which of the below configurations in calculate stage is correct to convert the string into date?

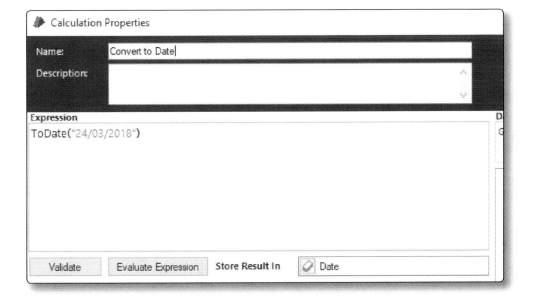

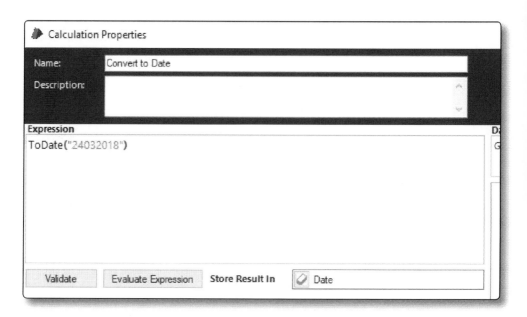

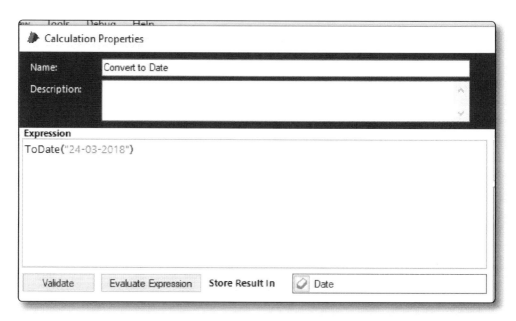

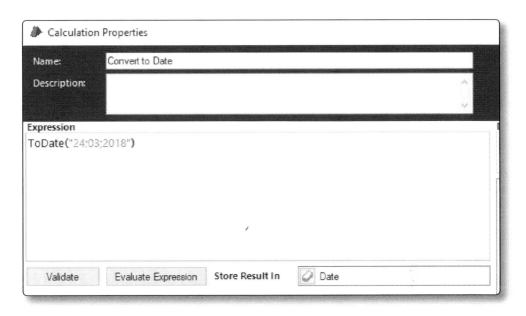

A. 1 and 2
B. 2 and 3
C. 1 and 3
D. 3 and 4

3. The action "Get Details" is defined as below.

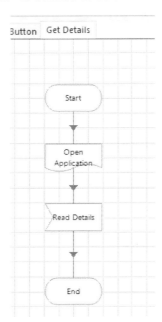

The properties of Open Application page are as below.

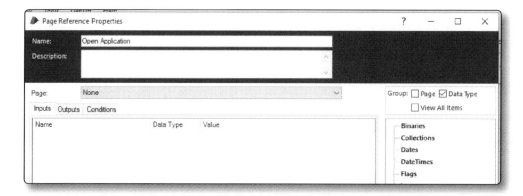

Which of the following statement is correct?

A. The execution of "Open Application" goes into infinite loop

B. The execution of "Open Application" pages throws exception

C. Blue Prism does not start the execution of "Get Details "action

D. None of the above

4. Which of the following spying mode has "Activate Application" action available in navigate stage for its elements?

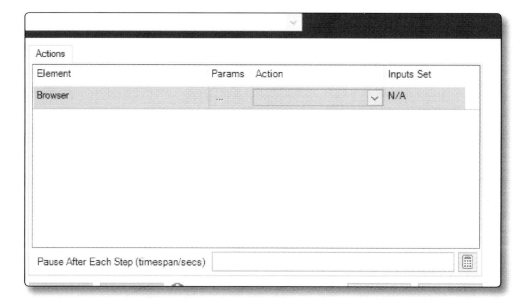

A. Active Accessibility (AA).

B. Win 32

C. Region

D. HTML

5. Blue Prism work queue has some exception cases with "Automatically set exception at clean up" as the exception reason. Which of the following caused this?

   A. Blue Prism has taken another case from queue before declaring the previous case as completed or exception

   B. A resume stage was not encountered when in recovery mode

   C. No exception block was not mentioned in the code

   D. Developer mentioned "Automatically set exception at clean up" as exception reason in mark as exception

6. Which part of the Blue Prism Is used to create environmental variables?

   A. Control Room

   B. System Manager

   C. Process Studio

   D. Object Studio

7. Which of the below configuration in calculation stage is correct to get day after tomorrow date in Blue Prism process flow?

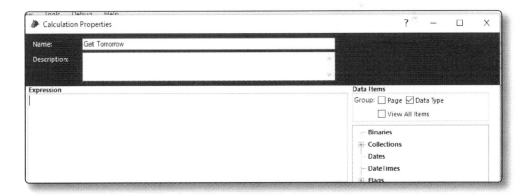

   A. AddDays(Today(), 2)

   B. AddDays(Today():2)

   C. Today()+2

   D. Tomorrow()

8. Which of the following statement describes a system exception in Blue Prism?

    A. A case that needs to be deleted from queue

    B. A case that was being processed when system is shutdown

    C. A case made an exception by process because it's outside of the scope

    D. A case cannot be completed cause of the unexpected system behaviour

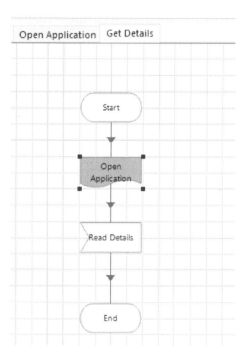

9. The current page stage is highlighted. The properties of current stage are as follows.

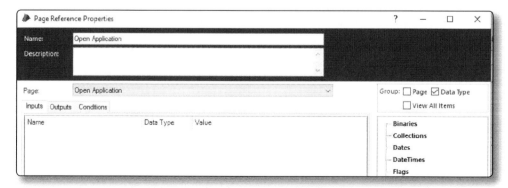

If developer does not want to execute the page "Open Application", what should he do?

A. Use the step (F11) or click 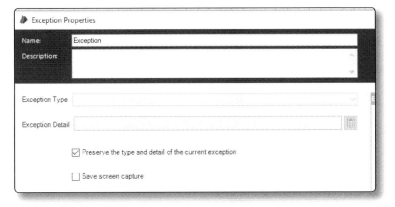 in process studio to navigate through the diagram

B. Use the step over (F10) or click button in process studio to step over the page "Open application"

C. Highlight "Read Details" stage and select "Set Next Stage"

D. It's not possible to skip the steps in the process when in execution

10. The properties of exception stage are as follows.

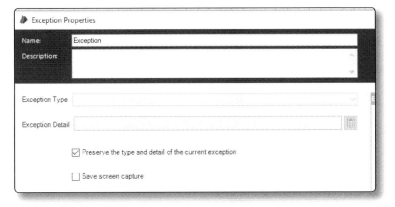

Which of the below configuration of a page is correct?

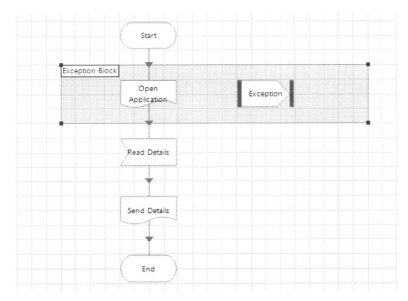

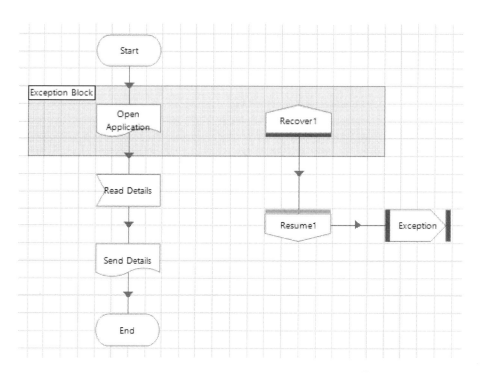

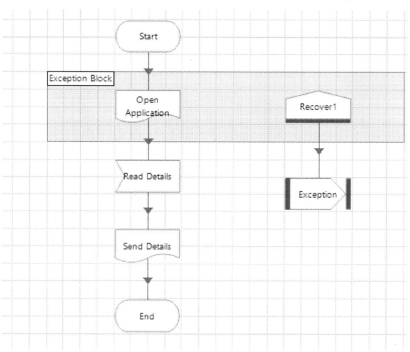

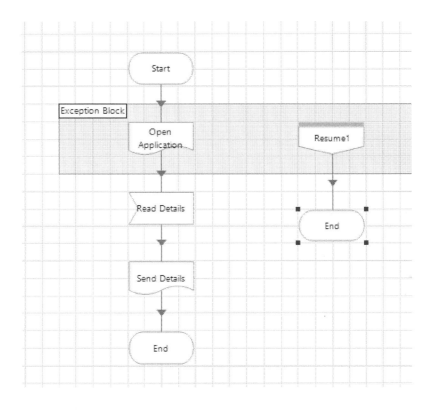

11. What Is the use of statistic variables in Blue Prism process?

    A. Statistic variables are used so that minor changes to the configuration of a solution can be made without the need make development changes to the objects or processes

    B. Statistic variables are used to change any configuration that may need changing whist a process session is running can be exposed as a Session variable

    C. Statistic variables are used to store the value of the data item in database for reporting purposes

    D. Statistic variables are not available in Blue Prism

12. Which of the below statements is incorrect about exception handling in Blue Prism?

    A. A page can only use one recover stage unless blocks are used

    B. Exceptions can be handled anywhere in business objects and processes

    C. A page can have multiple blocks, if they do not overlap

    D. Blocks can overlap, and blocks can be nested

13. A page is configured as below.

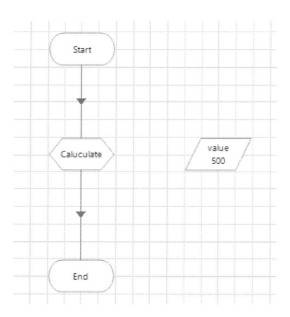

The number data Item "value" has 500 as initial value. The calculation stage is configured as below.

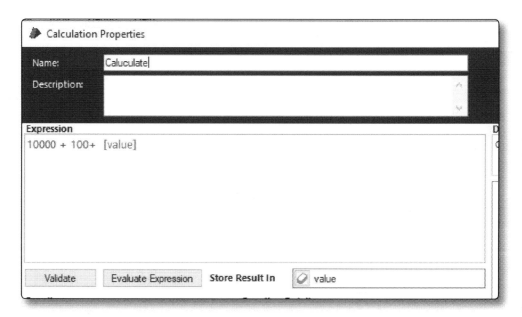

After execution of the calculate stage. Which of the following is true?

A. The data item "value" will contain 500

B. The data item "value" will contain 10100

C. Can't use + on number data Items

D. The data item "value" will contain 10600

14. Study the following process flow.

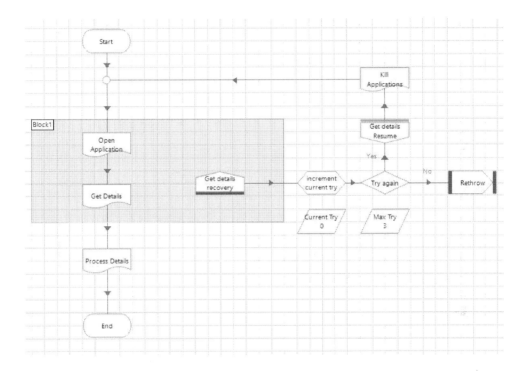

The process logic is designed to try three time before rethrowing the exception.

"Current try" is number data item with initial value 0.

"Max try" is a number data with initial value 3.

To enable this work correctly, what is the correct configuration for "Try Again" decision stage?

Decision Properties

Name: Try again

Description:

Expression

[Current Try] <= [Max Try]

Decision Properties

Name: Try again

Description:

Expression

[Current Try] >= [Max Try]

Decision Properties

Name: Try again

Description:

Expression

[Max Try] <= [Current Try]

15. Which of the below statements explains what Blue Prism is used for?

    A. Blue Prism is used for data flow
    B. Blue Prism is used for connecting the applications
    C. Blue Prism is used for creating robots that can replicate user actions
    D. Blue Prism has no use

16. There is requirement that process can be stopped from the control room whist the process is in execution. A flag data item called "stop ASAP" is used in the process flow. What exposure should be given to the "stop ASAP" data item?

    A. None
    B. Environment
    C. Session
    D. Statistic

17. Which property of the work queue is used to record how far through your process a work queue item has been worked?

    A. Tags
    B. Status
    C. Priority
    D. Attempt

18. Which of the following is not a wait stage condition?

    A. Check Window Attribute
    B. Check AA Attribute
    C. Check Region Attribute
    D. Check HTML Attribute

19. A process is configured as below.

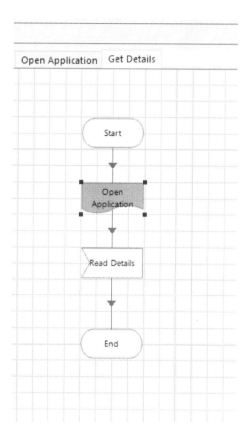

The current page stage is highlighted. The properties of current stage are as follows.

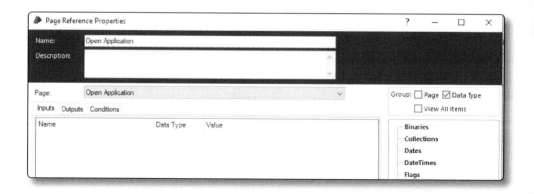

There are no break points configured in it.

What will be effect of pressing the step out ⌁ (shift and F11) button?

A. The process will step into the "Open Application" page and will pause on the start stage of the page

B. The Process will execute all the stages in the "Open Application" page and move on to the "read details" stage where it will pause

C. The Process will skip the processing "Open Application" page and move on to the "read details" stage where it will pause

D. The process will execute all the stages on the current page and pause on the page that called the current page.

20. Which of the following is true if sensitive data needs to be saved in work queue as Item Key?

A. "Key" field of the queue should be encrypted with credential key

B. "Key Name" parameter of the work queue should not be configured

C. High Priority should be given to all the cases

D. Work Queue internally encrypts everything. Don't need to do anything explicitly.

21. A process has been created but it is not listed in control room to run on another machine. Which of the below scenario that may suggest why?

A. The process uses objects with different run modes

B. The process is only created to run from process studio

C. The process has not been published

D. Process has more than 99 errors in code

- 1 and 2

- 3 only

- 1,2 and 3

- Any of the scenarios

22. How many end stages can one page have?

A. 1
B. 2
C. Any number
D. 0

23. Which of the below functionality does system manager module of BP (Blue Prism) provide?

A. Managing Web Services
B. Managing Work Queues
C. Roles Management
D. All the above

24. An action called "application-login" fails with following exception

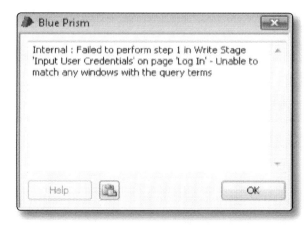

What might have caused the above exception?

A. The element used in the Input User Credentials stage could not be found in the application
B. "Input User Credentials" stage could find multiple elements conflicting with the element referenced in "Input User Credentials" stage
C. "Input User Credentials" stage is trying to attach to application
D. An action "Input User Credentials" does not exist on the page "Log In"

25. Which of the following stages does not accept the out bound link in Blue Prism?

A. Start Stage
B. End Stage
C. Navigate Stage
D. Alert Stage

26. An object page is configured to enter user name and password to login to application. When the user name and password elements are spied, the finger print (attributes) are identical except the Windows text element.

The values of windows text elements are username for username text box, password for password textbox.

The user name element has the below attribute set:

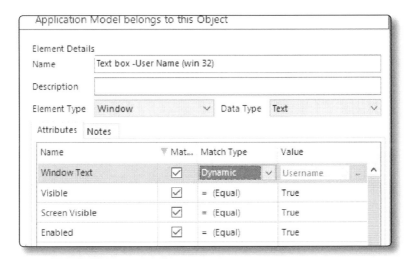

A write stage has been configured to enter user name.

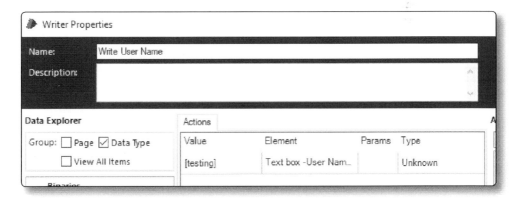

What additional configuration is require selecting the username textbox?

A. None, the element username is already selected in Application Modeller

B. The "params" button should be selected and the parameter configured to over write windows text should be set as "Username"

C. Two elements should be created for password and username

D. Write stage automatically detects the element based on the value that is passed

27. What stage in object studio is used to launch application?

A. Read
B. Navigate
C. Attach
D. Write

28. An object is configured to enter data into a form of application. When elements are spied, they have exactly same foot print(attributes). Which of the below attribute should be used to uniquely identify those elements?

A. Match Index
B. Match Reverse
C. Name
D. Value

29. Which of the following is not an application modeller match type Operator? Refer the below application modeller.

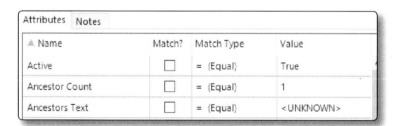

A. Dynamic
B. * (Wild Card)
C. .*(Reg ex)
D. Substring

30. Which of the following statement is incorrect?

A. Single bot can work on a queue, at one point of time
B. Queued cased can be monitored from control room
C. Multiple robots can work on same queue
D. Work queue can be used to share the work load among robots

31. A process needs to interact with Java application. Which of the below component should be installed prior to spying the java application?

   A. Java Access Bridge
   B. SQL database
   C. Windows Access
   D. None of the above

32. Which of the following is the correct syntax to use a data item in an expression?

   A. {Data Item}
   B. "Data Item"
   C. [Data Item]
   D. (Data Item)

33. Which of the given configuration should be used to focus a running application.

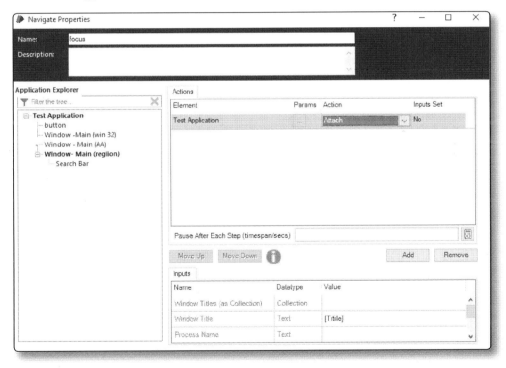

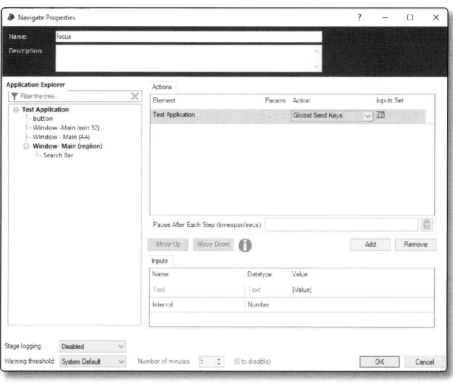

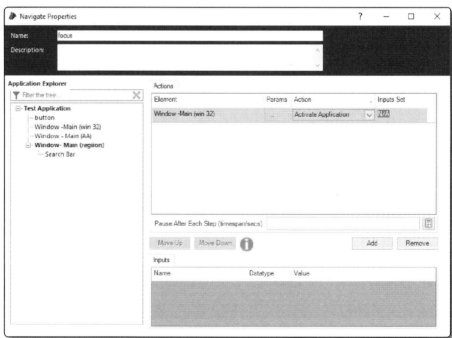

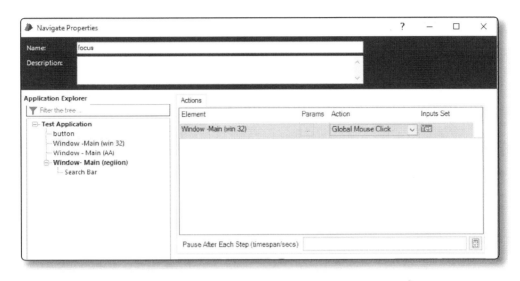

34. How many application manager modes are available in blue Prism?

    A. 1

    B. 5

    C. 3

    D. 4

35. A process is configured as below.

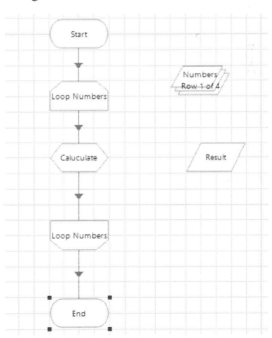

The properties of collection Numbers is as follows.

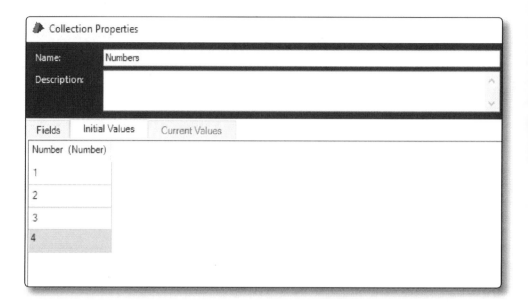

Calculation stage is configured as shown in below image.

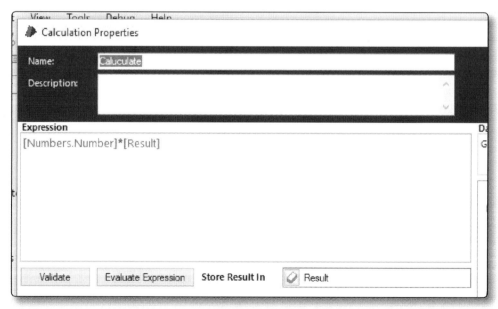

Date item result is defined as below.

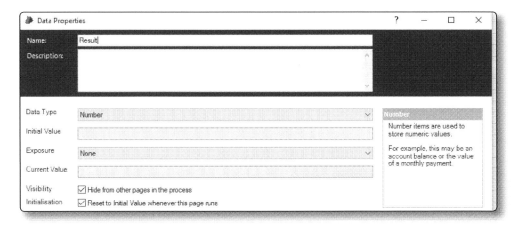

What value will be saved in data item result after the execution of the page?

A. 24

B. 48

C. 96

D. Exception will be thrown

36. A process is configured as below.

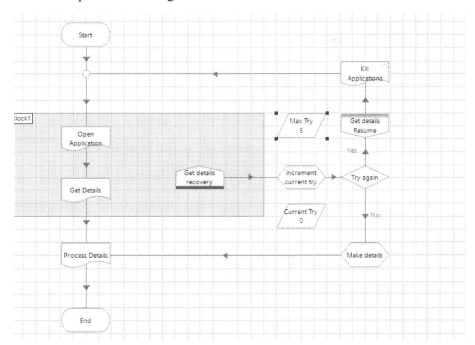

What problem is there in the process design?

A. Retry limit is configured to 5 when it should always be 3
B. There is missing resume stage on one of the routes through exception flow
C. Recovery logic should be in exception block
D. Process is configured well

37. In Blue prism work queue what does the 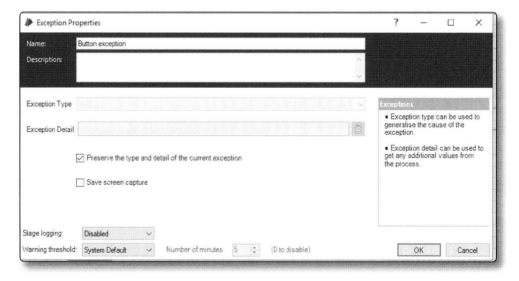 represent?

A. The case has been worked successfully
B. The case has encountered an exception and needs manual intervention
C. The case is currently being worked
D. The case is pending to be worked

38. Study the following diagram of the exception properties.

Consider the following scenarios.

- This exception stage throws system exception if its not placed in recover flow.

- This exception stage throws a new system exception with the details of button exception which was raised already.

- The exception stage will not be logged in session log

- All above

Which of the statements are true?

A. 1 and 3
B. Only 2
C. 2 and 3
D. 4 only

39. If a case is in being worked by robot, which of the following symbols is used to mark the case?

A.
B.
C.
D.

40. The order number input field has been spied in Blue Prism.

The following attributes have been returned by application modeller.

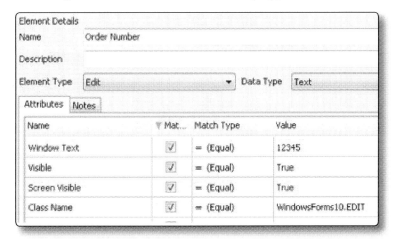

What attribute should be unchecked to ensure the consistent visibility of element?

A. Windows Text
B. Visible
C. Screen Visible
D. Class Name

41. Which of the following statement is true about run mode of the object?

A. Setting the run mode to background will enable the object to run at the same time as fore ground or back ground objects on the same machine
B. Setting the run more to fore ground will give the object priority over any other business object
C. Setting run mode to exclusive ensure only one process runs on the resource.
D. Run mode can be left blank

42. Study the following page.

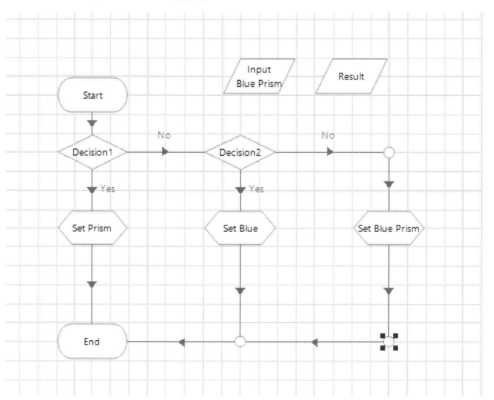

Decision Properties

Name: Decision1

Description:

Expression

InStr([Input], "Prism")=0

Decision Properties

Name: Decision2

Description:

Expression

StartsWith([Input], "Blue")

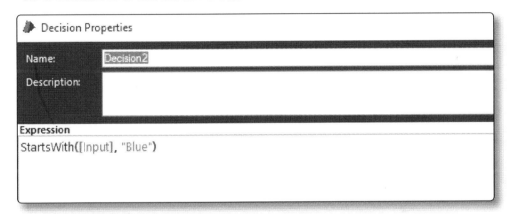

Calculation Properties

Name: Set Prism

Description:

Expression

"Prism"

| Validate | Evaluate Expression | Store Result In | Result |

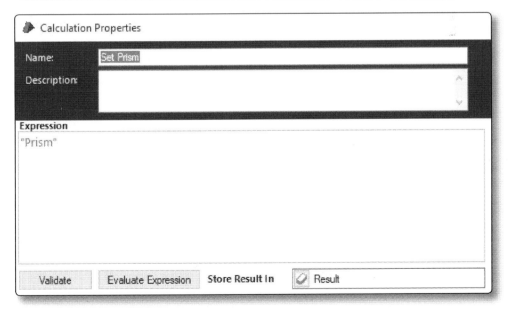

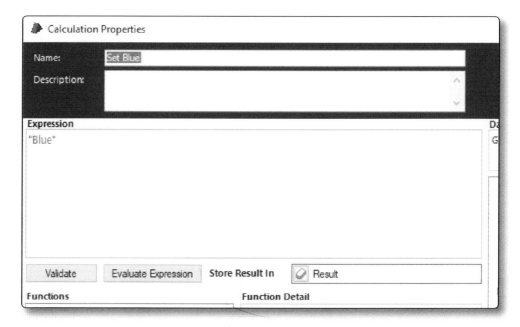

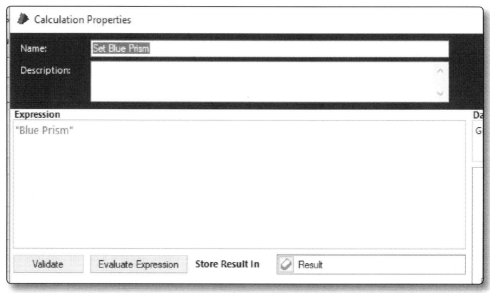

What value would be stored after page has run?

A. Blue

B. Prism

C. Blue Prism

D. An internal exception will be thrown

43. A Process is configured as below.

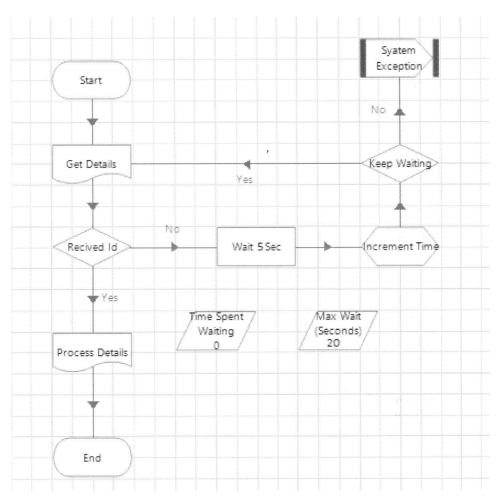

The process is intended to wait for 5 seconds each time the "Get Details" stage does not retrieve ID for up to 20 secs before throwing an exception.

Data Item "Max Wait(seconds)" is a number data item with an initial value of 20.

Data Item "Time Spent Waiting" is a number data item with an initial value of 0.

To enable this to work correctly, what Is the below configuration for the "Increment Time" calculation stage?

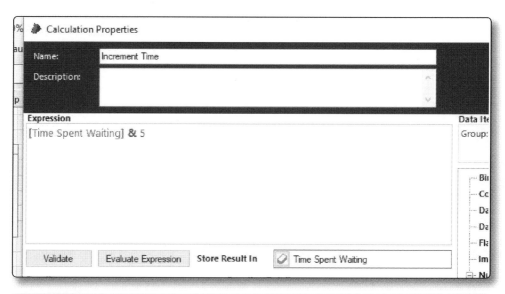

Name:	Increment Time
Description:	

Expression   Da

(Time Spent Waiting) + 5   G

Validate	Evaluate Expression	**Store Result In**	🖉 Time Spent Waiting

44. Study the below flow.

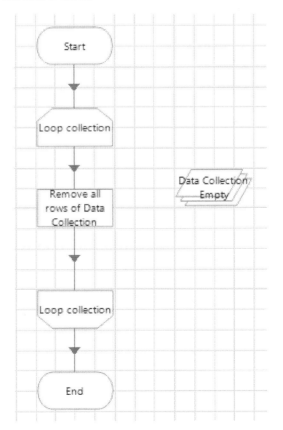

Which of the following statement is true?

A. Internal exception will be thrown

B. Blue Prism does not start the execution

C. Process will not initiate any new iteration and continue to end stage

D. Process gets terminated with system exception

45. Which part of the blue prism is used to create the work queues?

A. Process Studio

B. Object Studio

C. Control Room

D. System Manager

46. Which of the blue prism feature is used to dynamically start the process based on queue load?

A. Queue Management

B. Active Queues

C. Scheduler

D. Session Management

47. Which of the following is not a Blue Prism internal object?

A. Work Queues

B. Collections

C. Credentials

D. Webservices-Rest

48. Which of the following object should be used to split the collections?

A. Utility-Collection Manipulation

B. Utility-General

C. Internal Business Objects- collections

D. Utility-Environment

49. How many tags can be added to a case in a work queue?

A. Only 1

B. More than 3

C. Less than 10

D. Any number

50. Which of the below statement explains RPA (Robotic Process Automation)?

A. RPA (Robotic Process Automation) is technology to read excel and input into the applications

B. RPA (Robotic Process Automation) is data entry technology

C. Robotic Automation refers to process automations where computer software drives existing enterprise application software in the same way that a user does

D. RPA is subpart of artificial intelligence

51. Which of the below switch is used to run the resourcepc in public mode?

A. Public
B. ResourcePC
C. Dbconname
D. Automate

52. What is the default visibility of the data items created on pages?

A. Global
B. Static
C. Local
D. Session

53. Study the properties of data items.

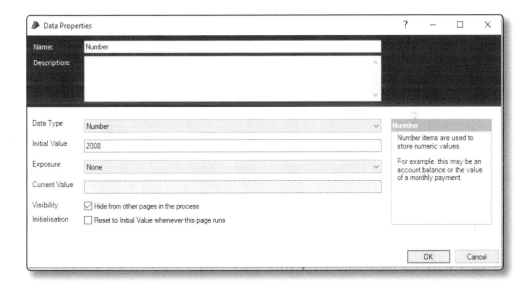

Which of the following statements is true?

A. Number data items is configured as global variable
B. Number data item is configured as session variable
C. Number data item is configured to save the year
D. Number data item holds the value from last execution of the page

54. Which of the below is not a data item of Blue Prism?

  A. Timespan

  B. Binary

  C. Flag

  D. Byte

55. Study the below image.

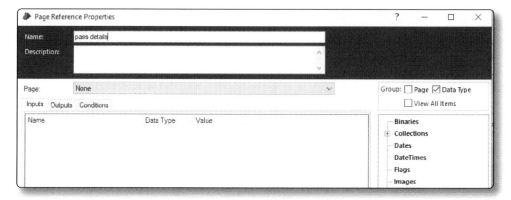

Which of the following statements is correct?

  A. Page "pass details" is referring to deleted page

  B. Page "pass details" is referring to page of another object

  C. Page "pass details" is refereeing to an action instead of page

  D. None of the above

56. In a process below exception was raised.

What does this exception indicate?

A. Business object is trying to access the application which is closed
B. Business object is trying to attach application which is already connected
C. Business object is trying to launch application which is already launched by object
D. Business objects is trying to activate the application which is minimized

57. Which of the following stages has neutral effect in the execution of the process?

A. Anchor
B. Action
C. Page
D. Link

58. The stage which can be used to throw exception in Blue Prism is called?

A. Exception Stage
B. Resume Stage
C. Recover Stage
D. None of the options

59. Which of the below actions are mandatory actions in Business Object?

A. Initialise and clean up
B. Login and logout
C. Launch and terminate
D. No actions are mandatory

60. Which of the below work queues object's action is used to get the pending case from work queue to be worked?

A. Get Pending Items
B. Get Item Data
C. Get Next Item
D. Get Locked Item

61. What is true about defer items from the work queue?

A. New cases can be deferred to prevent them from being worked
B. Defer means the items are temporarily frozen
C. If get next item does not get an item, it does not necessarily mean that there are no unworked items in the queue
D. All the above

62. Which of the following is the correct configuration in calculate stage to get the last date of the current month?

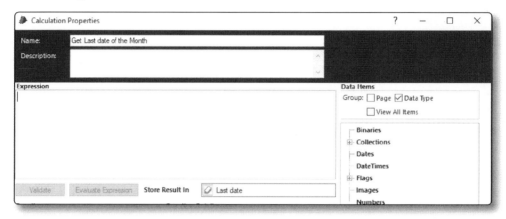

A. AddDays(AddMonths(MakeDate(01; Mid(Today(); 4; 2); Mid(Today(); 7; 4));1), -1)

B. MakeDate(01; Mid(Today(); 4; 2); Mid(Today(); 7; 4))

C. AddDays(MakeDate(01; Mid(Today(); 4; 2); Mid(Today(); 7; 4)), -1)

D. None of the above

63.

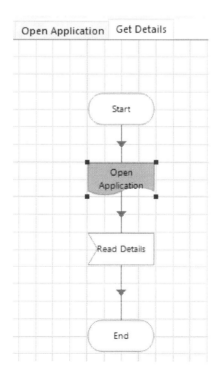

The current page stage is highlighted. The properties of current stage are as follows.

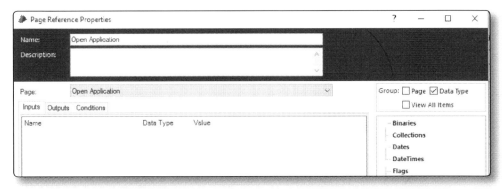

If developer does want to debug the page "Open Application", what should he do?

A. Use the step (F11) or click in process studio to navigate through the diagram

B. Use the step over (F10) or click button in process studio to step over the page "Open application"

C. Highlight "Read Details" stage and select "Set Next Stage"

D. It's not possible to skip the steps in the process when in execution

64. How long does change in the session variable take to reflect in the process?

A. Immediately

B. After restarting the Blue Prism

C. After restarting the machine

D. Never, values can't be changed once created

65. Which of the below statement explains exception bubbling?

A. Terminating the process with exception

B. An exception moves upward through the layers of a solution(sub-pages) is known as bubbling

C. Usage of exception Blocks

D. Nullifying the exception with resume stage

66. An exception was thrown because the system provided the message: "User does not exist". What type of the exception is this?

A. System Exception

B. Business Exception

C. Validation Exception

D. None of the above

67. A process is defined as below.

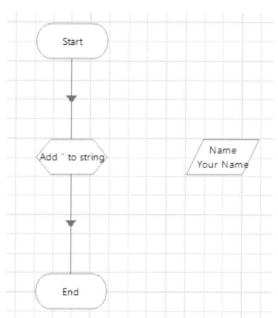

Which of the below configuration is correct to add "(Double quote) to a string data item "Name" in calculation stage "Add "to string""?

A. """" & [Name] & """"
B. """" + [Name] + """"
C. Chr(034)& [Name] & Chr(034), 034 is being the ASCII value of "
D. Chr(034) + [Name] + Chr(034), 034 is being the ASCII value of "

68. When is otherwise stage of choice stage executed?

A. When all the choices of choice stage are correct
B. When all the choices of choice stage are incorrect
C. When choice stage has otherwise choices configured
D. Otherwise stage is never executed

69. Which of the following is not correct about wait stage?

A. A wait stage can wait for a single condition or several conditions
B. A wait stage can exist without any condition and the timeout can be used as a pause
C. An exception at the timeout stage will alert the process to an error that has happened
D. "Time out" of wait stage should be a whole number

70. A Process is configured as follows.

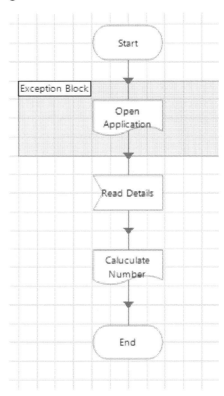

Read details stage reads the bank account number from target application. User wants not to show the account in logs. What should be done to skip the logging of bank account number?

A. Stage logging on read stage should be disabled or changed to errors only

B. Logging should be disabled on the execution machine of the process

C. Bank account number should be saved in password type data item

D. Blue Prism automatically detects the sensitive data like bank accounts, credit card number etc.

71. Which of the following parts of Blue Prism is used for running a process on virtual robot?

A. Process studio

B. Control Room

C. Object Studio

D. Application Modeller

72. A process is configured as below.

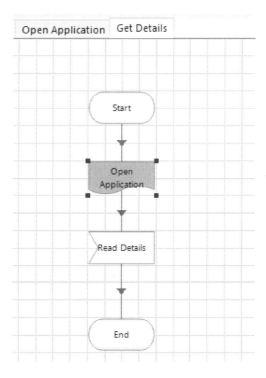

The current page stage is highlighted. The properties of current stage are as follows.

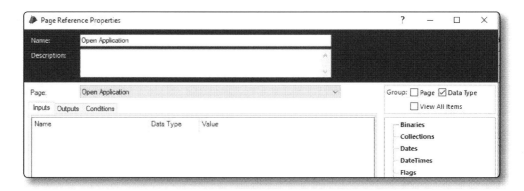

There are no break points configured in it.

What will be effect of pressing the step ⧉ (F11) button?

   A. The process will step into the "open Application" page and will pause on the start stage of the page

   B. The Process will execute all the stages in the "open Application" page and move on to the "read details" stage where it will pause

   C. The Process will skip the processing "open Application" page and move on to the "read details" stage where it will pause

   D. The process will execute all the stages on the current page and pause on the page that called the current page

73. Which stage(s) can be configured in process to send Input and output parameters to another page or another process?

   A. Start stage

   B. End stage

   C. None of the above

   D. Both start and end stage

74. An action called "Activate Window" fails with following exception.

What might have caused the above exception?

   A. The element used in the Input User Credentials stage could not be found in the application

   B. "Activate Window" stage could find multiple elements conflicting with the element referenced in "Input User Credentials" stage

   C. ""Activate Window"" stage is trying to attach to application

   D. An action "Activate Window" is not does not exist on the page

75. Which of the following stages should not be used in exception block?

A.

B.

C.

D.

76. When should reset button in process studio be used?

A. After re-running the process

B. Before re-running the process

C. Either before running or after running the process

D. Not necessary to use

77. A process is configured to send password to target test application as below.

Which of the following statements is correct?

A. Process will fail because to write password, write stage should be used

B. The application should be in focus and cursor should be in password field for the navigate stage to be successful

    C. The stage will fail – data items should not be used to send value to input parameter "Name"

    D. Process will execute successfully even the application is minimized

78. An object is configured to enter data into a form of application. When elements are spied, they have exactly same foot print(attributes), which of the below configuration is correct to identify first element?

    A. Match Index = 1, Match Revese = true

    B. Match Index = Number of elements, Match Revese = false

    C. Match Index = 1, Match Revese = false

    D. None of the above

79. Which of the below application mode can be used to attach to 64-bit application?

    A. Internal, 64-bit mode

    B. External, 64-bit mode

    C. External, OS address size

    D. External Blue Prism address size

80. Debugging can be done stage by stage in Blue Prism. Which of the below is used to traverse pages quickly?

    A. Step Over

    B. Step Out

    C. None of them

    D. Both A and B

81. An action in the process is failed with following error.

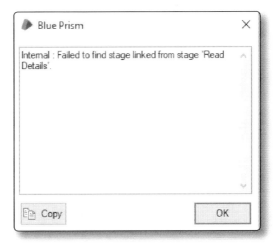

What does the exception indicate?

A. An internal error always indicates product failure
B. Read stage is not connected to any other stage
C. Application is not launched
D. Read details stage is no longer existed in Business object

82. In Blue prism work queue what does the ▶ represent?

A. The case has been worked successfully
B. The case has encountered an exception and needs manual intervention
C. The case is currently being worked
D. The case is pending

83. When attempting to run a process in control room the following message appears.

Not connected to BP0008 - can't start process

Consider the following scenario?

A. Resource BP0008 is not responding to request Blue Prism from control room
B. Resource BP0008 is offline
C. Resource BP0008 is shutdown
D. Resource BP0008 is running a process with exclusive object

Which of the above scenarios would invoke the message?

A. 1 only
B. 4 only
C. 2 or 3
D. 2,3 and 4

84. A Process is configured as below.

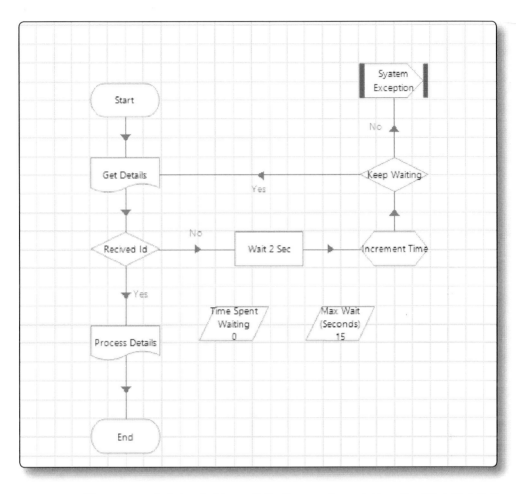

The process is intended to wait for 2 seconds each time the "Get Details" stage does not retrieve ID for up to 20 secs before throwing an exception.

Data Item "Max Wait(seconds)" is a number data item with an initial value of 20.

Data Item "Time Spent Waiting" is a number data item with an initial value of 0.

To enable this to work correctly, what Is the below configuration for the "Keep Waiting" decision stage?

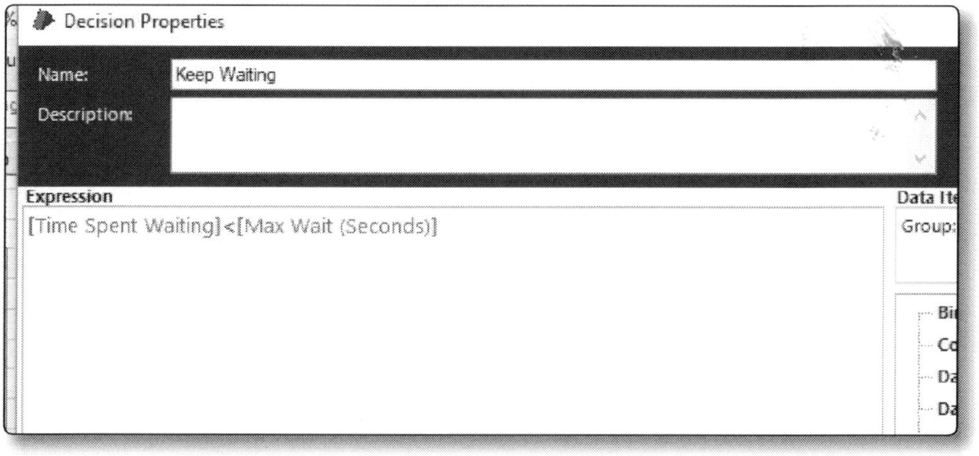

Decision Properties

Name:	Keep Waiting
Description:	

Expression

[Time Spent Waiting]<[Max Wait (Seconds)]

Data It

Group:

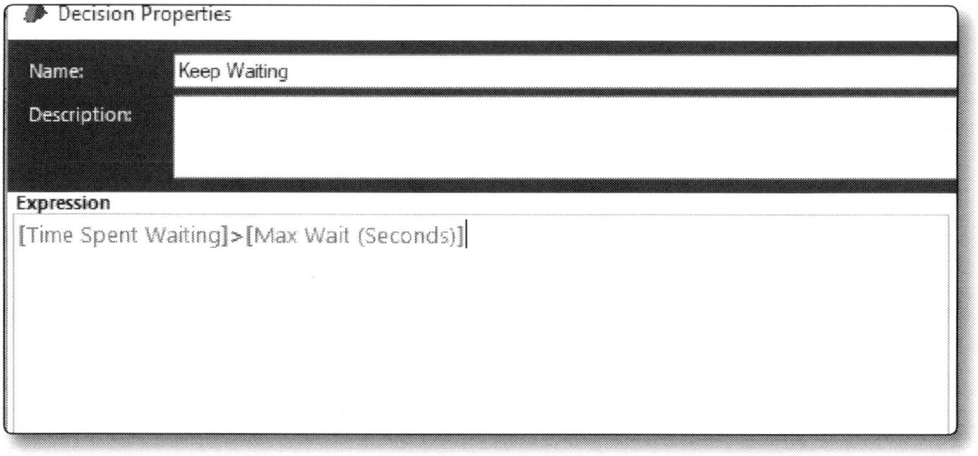

Bi
C
Da
Da

Decision Properties

Name:	Keep Waiting
Description:	

Expression

[Time Spent Waiting]>[Max Wait (Seconds)]

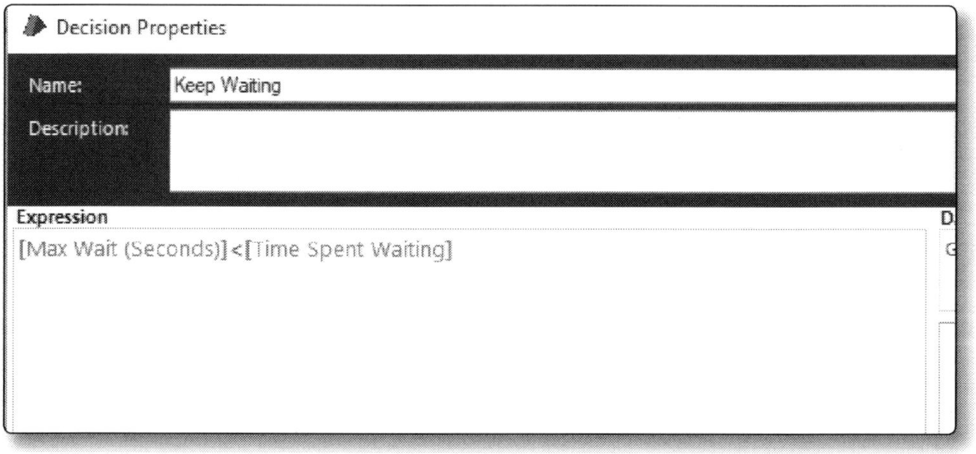

Decision Properties

Name:	Keep Waiting
Description:	

Expression

[Max Wait (Seconds)]<[Time Spent Waiting]

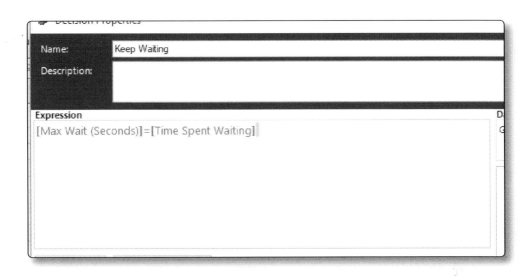

85. Examine the following page:

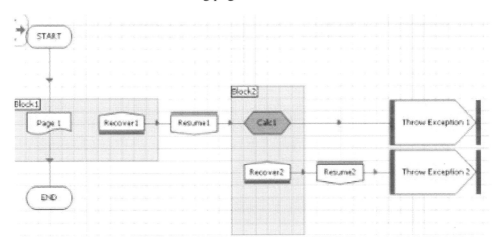

An error has occurred in page1 and the exception has bubbled up to be recovered in the recover1 stage. If there is an error in the calc1 stage which path will the process take?

A. The error will be recovered in recover2 stage

B. The error will cause to jump to end stage

C. The error will cause process to terminate

D. The process will continue to the throw exception1 stage

86. An action called "login" fails immediately with the following exception details.

System Exception : Login screen not found

When does this exception happen?

A. The action does not exist

B. The application has not launched

C. The action threw exception back to process

D. The action failed to navigate to login screen

87. Examine the below process flow.

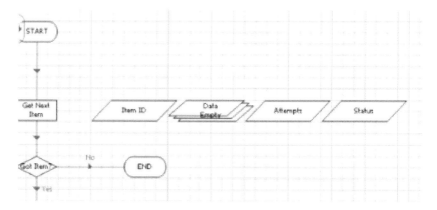

Get next item action output parameters are configures as follows.

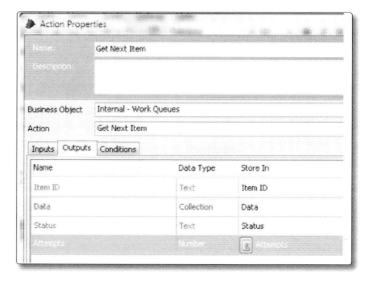

What is the correct configuration of the "Got Item" stage?

A. Item Id <> ""
B. Data <> ""
C. [Item ID] <>""
D. [Data] <>""

88. Which of the following action of Internal Business Objects- work queues should be used to add cases to work queues?

A. Get next item
B. Add to Queue
C. Set Data
D. Defer

89. Which of the blue prism feature is used to configure the process executions?

A. Queue Management
B. Active Queues
C. Scheduler
D. Session Management

90. Which of the below configuration is correct to make the data item "Age" a global data item?

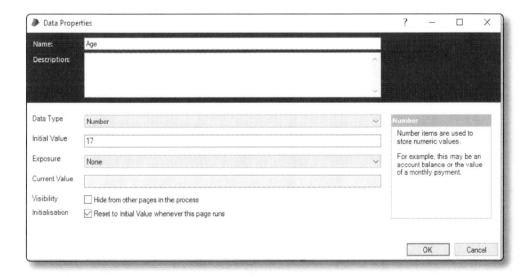

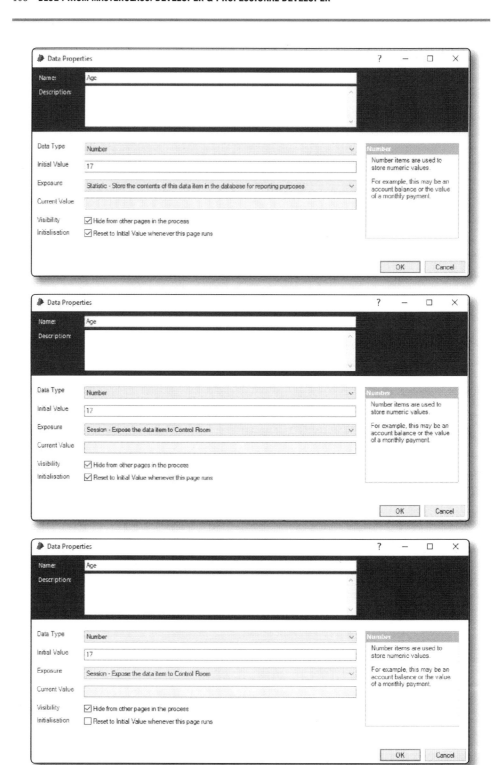

91. How are collection properties in Blue Prism accessed?

   A. Collection Name.Field Name

   B. Collection Name-Field Name

   C. 'Collection Name.Field Name'

   D. "Collection Name.Field Name"

92. In a process below exception was raised.

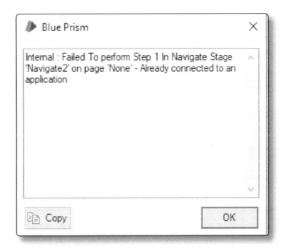

What does this exception indicate?

   A. Business object is trying to access the application which is closed

   B. Business object is trying to attach application which is already connected

   C. Business object is trying to launch application which is already launched by object

   D. Business objects is trying to activate the application which is minimized

93. 10 debug points are configured in Process flow. What is the effect of breakpoints if process is being executed from control room on a virtual robot?

   A. Process runs and breakpoints are ignored

   B. Process runs and process stops at break points

   C. Process does not start execution on virtual robot

   D. Process is not visible in control room if break points are configured

94. Which of the below is a default page in Blue Prism process?

   A. Mark as completed

   B. Mark as exception

   C. Main

   D. Load Queue

95. Consider the following statements.

   A. Stepping into an action stage will open object studio and stepping out will close it.

   B. Stepping into a process reference stage will open another Process Studio window

   C. A business object flows through pages one at a time

   D. A process uses an action stage to employ a business object page

Which of the above statements are correct?

   A. 1 and 2

   B. 2 and 3

   C. 3 and 4

   D. All the scenarios

96. Which of the following stage should follow the recovery stage?

   A. Alert

   B. Exception

   C. Exception Block

   D. Resume

97. Attach action is created as below in "test application object" to attach to application.

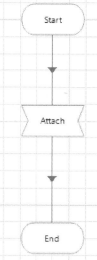

Properties of attach actions are as follows:

Which of the below statements is true about the attach action?

A. Attach action attaches to the application even if object tries to attach to the already connected application

B. Attach action throws exception if object tries to attach to the already connected application

C. Attach action launches the application if it's not already launched

D. Navigation stage should not be used to attach to application

98. In a process execution below error appeared.

What does the error indicate?

A. Process is trying to launch the application which is already launched
B. Process is trying to attach to the application which is already attached
C. Process is trying to attach to the application which is not launched
D. Process is not able to identify the window of the application

99. A page is created in business object but it's not available in process studio to be called using action stage? Which of the below statements may suggest why?

A. Page has compiler errors
B. Page has not been published
C. Page has been used in another page
D. Page has been configured invisible

    A. 1 and 2
    B. 2 only
    C. 2 and 3
    D. 3 and 4

100. A process has thrown below exception in its execution.

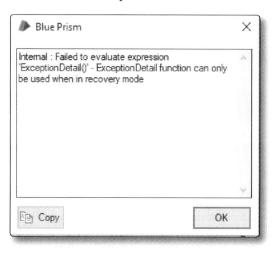

What does this exception indicate?

A. ExceptionDetail() function has been used in the main page
B. ExceptionDetail() function has been used in mark as exception page
C. ExceptionDetail () function has not been used in recovery mode i.e. in between a recover and a resume
D. ExceptionDetail () function has been used in recovery mode i.e. in between a recover and a resume

101. There is a requirement to create a new case for an exception case. Examine the properties of mark as exception action.

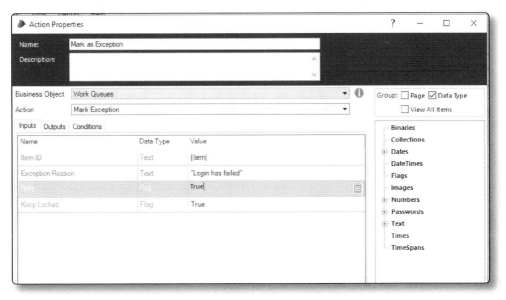

Which of the following statements is correct?

A. Current case is marked as exception and the new cloned item will become instantly locked

B. Current case is marked as exception and the new cloned items will not be locked

C. Current case is marked as completed and the new cloned item will become instantly locked

D. Current case is marked as completed and the new cloned items will not be locked

102. When attempting to run a process in control room the following message appears.

Consider the following scenario?

- Resource BP0008 is not responding to Blue Prism from control room
- Resource BP0008 is offline
- Resource BP0008 is shutdown
- Resource BP0008 is running a process with exclusive object

Which of the above scenarios would invoke the message?

A. 1 only

B. 4 only

C. 2 and 3

D. 2,3 and 4

103. Which of the below file types uses blue prism to export Processes or Business objects?

A. XML file

B. XSLT File

C. BPrealese file

D. Cs file

104. Which of the following statements is correct about environmental variable?

A. Environment variables are available to all processes and business objects

B. Data Items exposed as environment variables are read-only.

C. The name and type of the data item must match the environment variable

D. All the above

105. Examine the properties of session data item "Stop if user demands" which is configured in process called "Process Account Details".

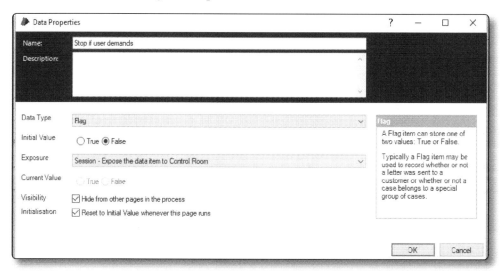

If two sessions of "Process Account Details" are being executed, which of the below statements is correct?

A. Change to session date item "Stop if user demands" would reflect in both sessions

B. Change to session date item "Stop if user demands" would reflect in the session which reads the date item first

C. Change to session date item "Stop if user demands" would reflect only in the one session and would not impact the "stop if user demands" variable of other session

D. None of the above

106. Which part of the blue prism is used to unlock the orphaned environmental locks?

A. Control Room

B. System Manager

C. Process Studio

D. Object Studio

107. A queue configuration is set to retry the exception item as follows.

And mark as exception action is configured as follows.

Which of the below statements is correct?

A. Current case is marked as exception and new clone is created

B. Current case is marked as exception and new clone is not created

C. Current case is not marked as exception and retries the same case

D. Current case is neither marked as exception nor marked as completed

108. Which of the following tools can be used to spy the mainframe applications?

    A. Grid Tool

    B. Java Access Bridge

    C. Active Accessibility API

    D. Spy ++

109. Which of the below methods should be used to respond to the request stop action from control room?

    A. GetSessionId()

    B. SingleSignon()

    C. IsStopRequested()

    D. IsImmediateStopRequested()

110. Which of the below stage is unique to process studio?

    A. ☐ Code

    B. ◯ Wait

    C. ▭ Read

    D. △ Alert

111. In a process, its required not to load duplicate cases into the queue. Which of the below configuration is correct to satisfy the requirement?

    A. Blue Prism work queues will never have duplicate cases by default

    B. "Get next item" action will not consider the duplicate cases if duplicate pending cases exist in queue

    C. "Is item in queue "should be called and should be verified if case not present in queue before adding it to queue

    D. Duplicate cases should be manually deleted from control room

112. Which of the following internal business object is used to perform operations on customized calendars of Blue Prism?

    A. Collections

    B. Scheduler

    C. Calendars

    D. Tasks

113. A read is configured as below exception and encountered exception in its execution.

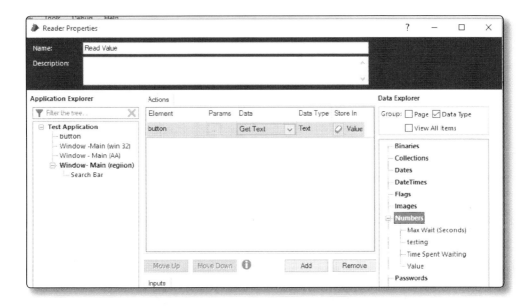

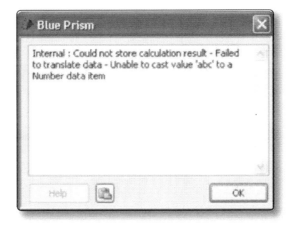

What may have caused the exception?

A. The Value data item already has the value defined in it

B. Value date item is of type Number and Blue failed to convert text to number

C. Button text should be "abcd"

D. Internal exception is caused by failure of Blue Prism application

114. What is the default port of Blue Prism resourcePc?

    A. 8000

    B. 8200

    C. 8181

    D. 8100

115.

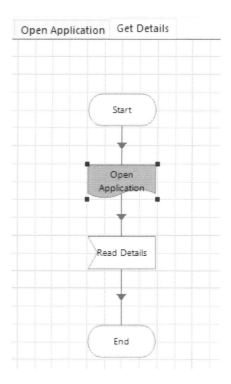

The current page stage is highlighted. The properties of current stage are as follows.

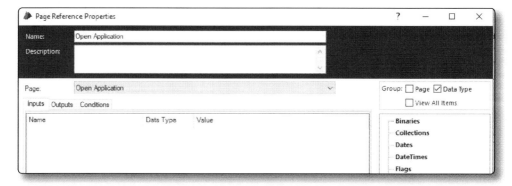

A debug point was set up at the start stage of page "open Application".

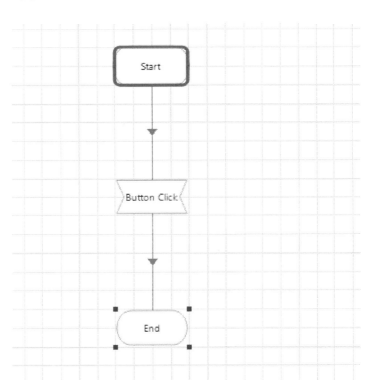

What will be effect of pressing the step over 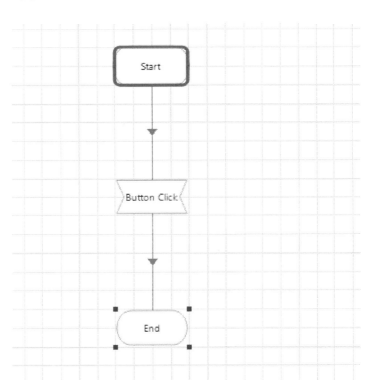 (F10) button?

A. The process will step into the "open Application" page and will pause on the start stage of the page

B. The Process will execute all the stages in the "open Application" page and move on to the "read details" stage where it will pause

C. The Process will skip the processing "open Application" page and move on to the "read details" stage where it will pause

D. The process will execute all the stages on the current page and pause on the page that called the current page.

116. Which of the Blue Prism component is used to login into virtual robot with robot user id?

A. Blue Prism Server

B. Login Agent

C. Resourcepc

D. ControllerPC

117. Examine the properties of read stage.

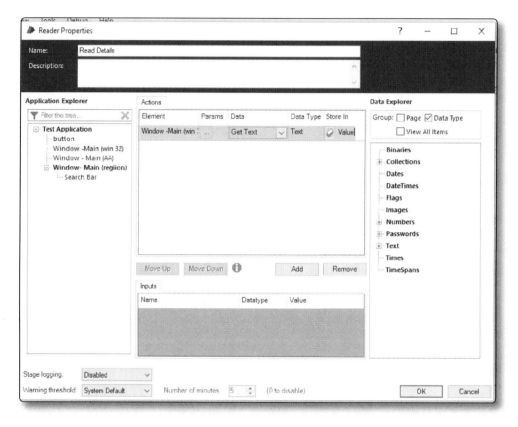

Which of the following statements is correct?

A. Stage logging should not be disabled for read stage

B. Warning status will be thrown in control room if read stage takes more than 5 minutes

C. Warning threshold is disabled on read stage

D. Blue Prism throws internal exception while executing this read stage

118. Which of the below is not a valid session status that's shown in control room?

A. Starting

B. Running

C. Pending

D. Completed

119. To create/modify process credentials, you would access.

- **A.** Control Room
- **B.** System
- **C.** Analytics
- **D.** Releases

120. Which of the native object is used to encrypt and decrypt the data items in Blue Prism flow?

- **A.** Credentials
- **B.** Work Queues
- **C.** Encryption
- **D.** None of the above

121. Which of the following can't be included in Environmental variables?

- **A.** Global timeout numbers for an application
- **B.** The URL for a browser-based application
- **C.** Email addresses for who email alerts should be emailed to
- **D.** Work Queue Data

122.

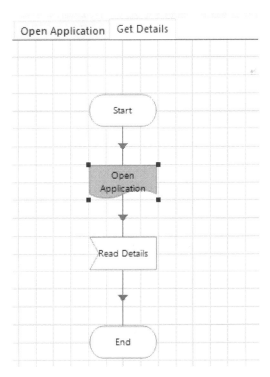

The Current page stage is highlighted. The properties of current stage are as follows:

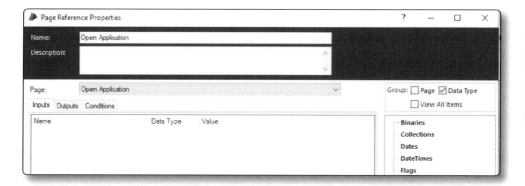

If developer does want to execute the page "Open Application" and does want to skip the debug, what should he do?

A. Use the step (F11) or click in process studio to navigate through the diagram

B. Use the step over (F10) or click button in process studio to step over the page "Open application"

C. Highlight "Read Details" stage and select "Set Next Stage"

D. It's not possible to skip the steps in the process when in execution

123. Which of the below statements is correct about IsStopRequested function?

A. IsStopRequested is used to check if Blue Prism process has end stage in its flow

B. IsStopRequested is used to stop process from Task Manager

C. IsStopRequested is used to check if a safe stop has been requested in the current session from Control Room

D. IsStopRequest is an action to notify user to stop the robot

124. Which of the below statements is correct about recovery stage?

A. Recovery stage should always be in exception block

B. Recovery stage without resume stage would throw error

C. Only one recovery stage should be used in process

D. Without Blocks, any extra recover stages than one on a page will be superfluous

125. Why to use Sub-Pages for?

     A. Readability and reusability
     B. Maintainability
     C. Better exception handling
     D. All the above

126. A process is configured as below.

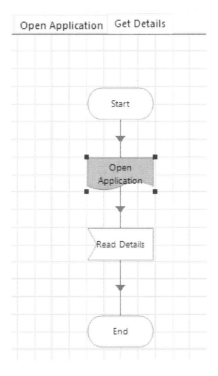

The current page stage is highlighted. The properties of current stage are as follows.

There are no break points configured in it.

What will be effect of pressing the step over ⌐⎯ (F10) button?

A. The process will step into the "open Application" page and will pause on the start stage of the page

B. The Process will execute all the stages in the "open Application" page and move on to the "read details" stage where it will pause

C. The Process will skip the processing "open Application" page and move on to the "read details" stage where it will pause

D. The process will execute all the stages on the current page and pause on the page that called the current page

127. What is action stage used for in Blue Prism?

A. It's used to call business object pages

B. It's used to perform actions on excel application

C. It's used to navigate through target application

D. It's used to launch the target application

128. An object is configured to enter data into a form of application. When elements are spied, they have exactly same foot print(attributes) which of the below configuration is correct to identify last element?

A. Match Index = 1, Match Reverse = true

B. Match Index = Number of elements, Match Reverse = true

C. Match Index = 1, Match Reverse = false

D. None of the above

129. Which part of the Blue Prism interacts with target application?

A. Control Room

B. Process Studio

C. Application Modeller

D. Object Studio

130. A process is configured as below.

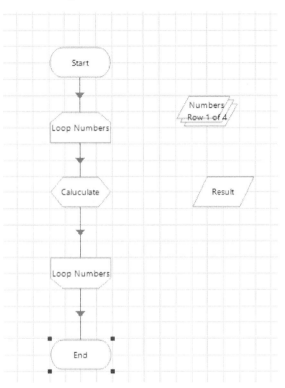

The properties of collection Numbers is as follows.

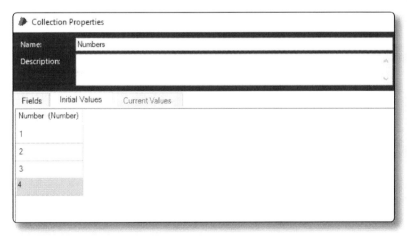

Calculation stage is configured as shown in below image.

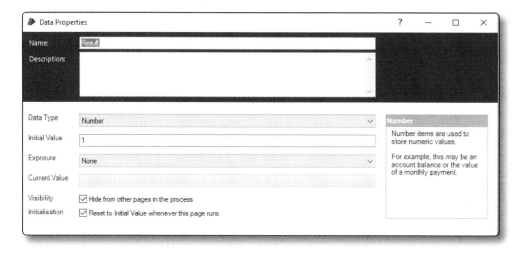

Date item result is defined as below.

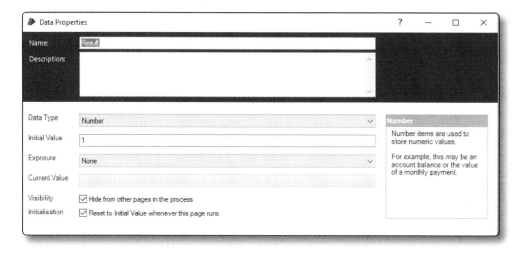

What value will be saved in data item result after the execution of the page?

A. 24

B. 48

C. 96

D. Exception will be thrown

131. Which of the following stage does not accept the inbound link in Blue Prism?

    A. End stage
    B. Start stage
    C. Navigate stage
    D. Alert stage

132. In Blue prism work queue what does the   ***   represent?

    A. The case has been worked successfully
    B. The case has encountered an exception and needs manual intervention
    C. The case is currently being worked
    D. The case is pending to be worked

133. Study the following page.

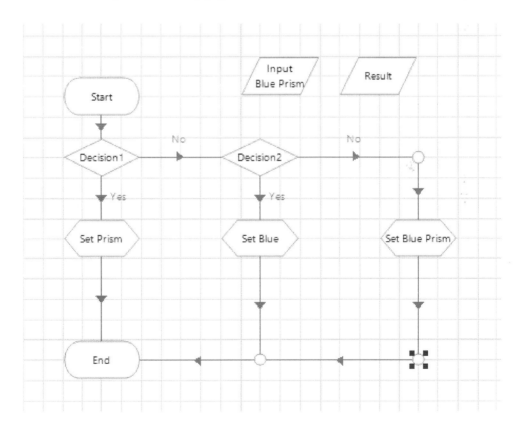

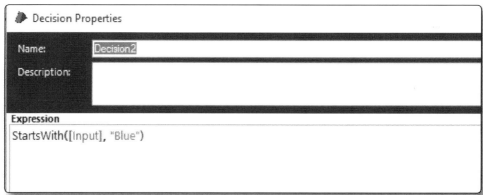

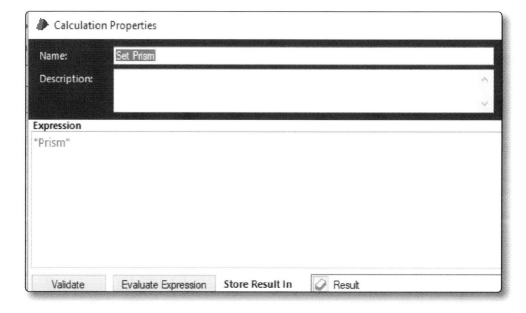

What value would be stored after page has run?

A. Blue
B. Prism
C. Blue Prism
D. An internal exception will be thrown

134. What is the default run mode of blue prism provided utility objects?

A. Foreground
B. Background
C. Exclusive
D. None

135. Which of the below is the name of the Blue Prism command line utility?

A. Public
B. ResourcePC
C. Dbconname
D. AutomateC

136. A process is designed to use collections.

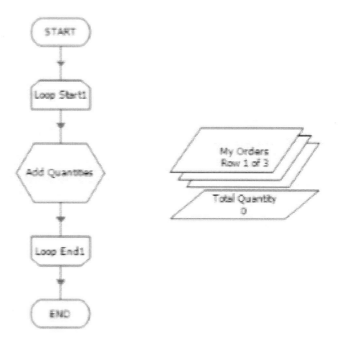

What is the correct configuration of calculation stage?

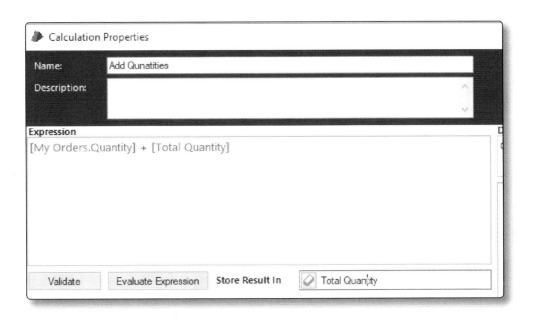

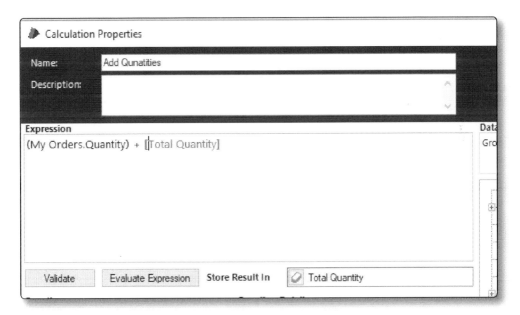

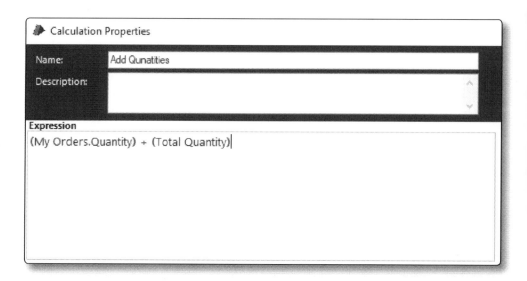

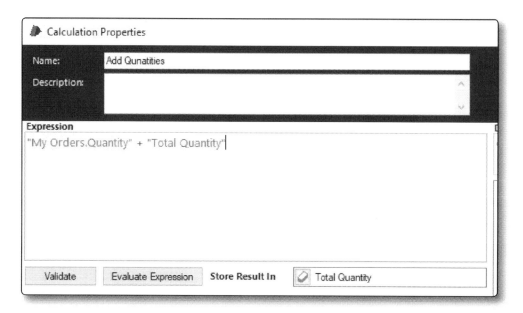

137. Which of the following is a Blue Prism internal object?

    A. Encryption
    B. Utility-Environment
    C. Utility-General
    D. Webservices-Rest

138. Which of the below configuration is correct to make the data item "age" a statistic data item?

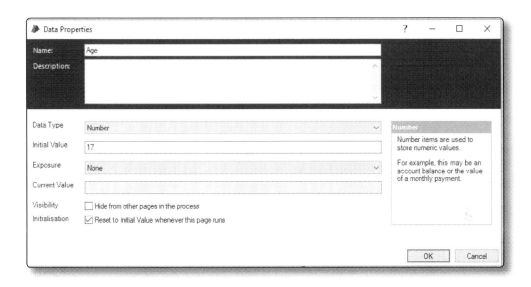

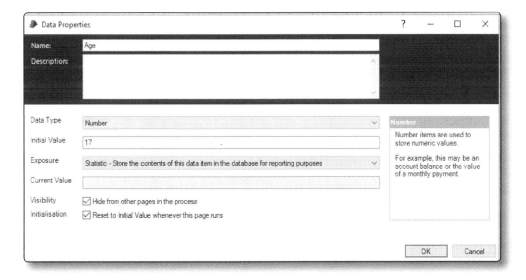

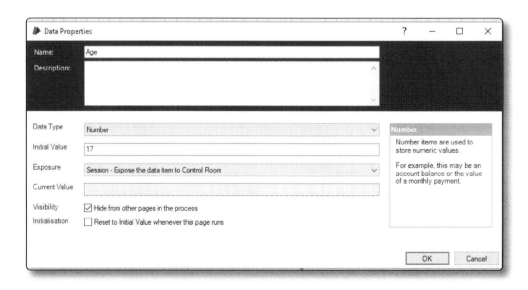

139. What is true about wait stage?

    A. A wait stage will take the path of the first True condition or, if the timeout elapses, the action can proceed to carry out further actions or as noted previously to throw an exception as "something" has not happened as expected

    B. An exception at the timeout stage will alert the Process to an error that has happened.

C. A wait stage can exist without any condition and the timeout can be used as a pause

D. All the above

140. Which of the following statements correct?

- Application logic is not contained in a Process

- A business object encapsulates the functionality of an application and exposes it to a process

- Process studio can directly interact with applications

- A business object is used to manipulate an application

A. 1 only
B. 2 and 3
C. 2,3 and 4
D. 1,2 and 4

141. A button click action is configured as follows.

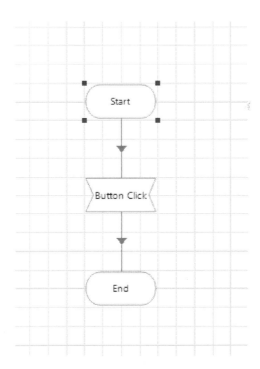

Properties of button click navigate stage is as below:

Which of the below statement is true about the Button click action?

A. "Button click" action fails if element "search bar" does not load on the application

B. "Button Click" action waits till "search bar" element appears before clicking on it

C. "Button Click" action gets executed successfully even "search bar" element is not loaded

D. None of the above

142. Examine the below image of properties of the action stage in a process.

Consider the following statements.

- Page "kill Applications" has been deleted from test object
- Page "kill Applications" has been unpublished from test object
- Page "kill Applications" has been renamed
- Page "Kill Applications" has been called in other page of the process

A. 1 and 2

B. 2 and 3

C. 1,2 and 3

D. 1,3 and 4

143. There is a requirement to create a new case for an exception case. Examine the properties of mark as exception action.

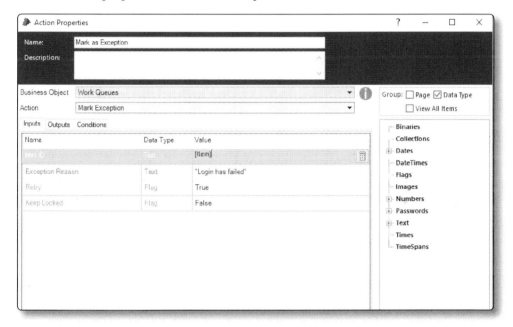

Which of the following statement is correct?

A. Current case is marked as exception and the new cloned item will become instantly locked

B. Current case is marked as exception and the new cloned items will not be locked and available as free item

C. Current case is marked as completed and the new cloned item will become instantly locked

D. Current case is marked as completed and the new cloned items will not be locked

144. Which of the following statement/s is/are correct?

A. When a business object launches an application, it is attached automatically.

B. Attach will fail if the business object is already attached

C. Attach needs an input value to help it identify the application.

D. All the above

145. An action in the process is failed with following error

> Internal : Failed to perform step 1 in Read Stage 'Read Details' on page 'Get Quote Details' - Not Connected

What does the exception indicate?

A. An internal error always indicates product failure

B. Read stage is not connected to any other stage

C. The business object is not connected to application either by launching it or attaching to it

D. Read details stage is no longer existed in business object

146. Which of the following statement is correct about Session variable?

A. Session Variables need no set-up in System Manager

B. Data Items exposed as Session Variables are writable

C. Session Variables can be viewed and modified from Control Room

D. All the above

147. Which of the below is not application connector of Blue Prism?

A. Windows application

B. Java-based application

C. Mainframe Application

D. Data Base application

148. A queue configuration is set to retry the exception item as follows.

And mark as exception action is configured as follows.

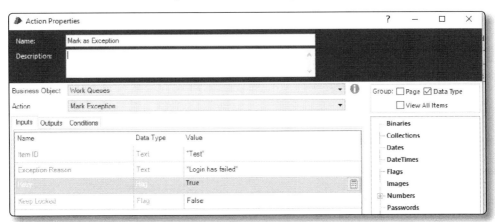

Which of the below statement is correct?

A. Current case is marked as exception and new clone is created

B. Current case is marked as exception and new clone is not created

C. Current case is not marked as exception and retries the same case

D. Current case is neither marked as exception nor marked as completed

149. Which of the below file types uses blue prism to create the release?

A. XML file

B. XSLT File

C. BPrelease file

D. Cs file

150. Study the following properties of "Add To Queue" action.

What will be the priority of the case that would be added to queue?

A. 5

B. 2

C. 3

D. 0

151. Acquire lock is configured as below in a process.

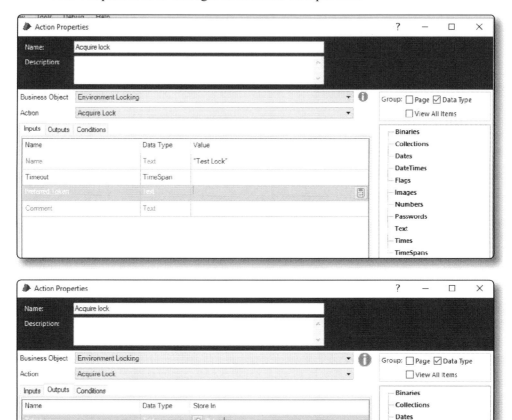

After the action acquire lock is executed, Token Data item is having no value.

Which of the below statements is true?

A. "Acquire Lock "action failed with internal exception

B. "Preferred Token" input variable Is mandatory for "Acquire lock "action

    C. Lock is already acquired by other session

    D. None of the above

152. How many start stages can one page have?

    A. 1

    B. 2

    C. Any number

    D. Page does not have start stage

153. Which of the below statement explains the application time out?

    A. This parameter determines how long Blue Prism waits for the target application to respond before throwing an exception

    B. This parameter defines how long blue prism waits to launch the application

    C. This parameter defines how long blue prism waits to send keys to application

    D. None of the above

154. Why alert stage is used in process flow?

    A. To raise exceptions

    B. To raise bespoke process alerts at strategic points in a process

    C. To make string calculations

    D. To make collections calculations

155. Blue Prism data base is configured to use active directory groups. Which of the following configuration is correct in calculation stage to derive if data base is configured to use active directory groups?

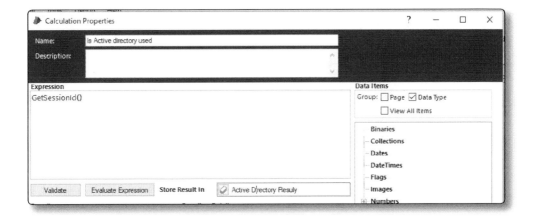

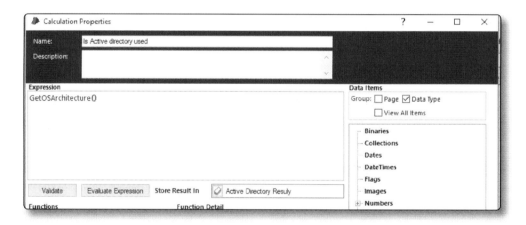

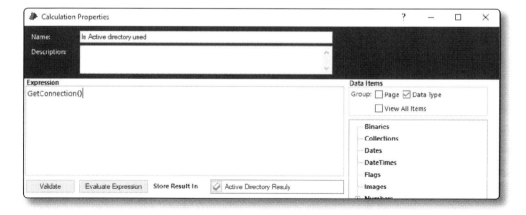

156. Which of the below connection type should be configured to use Blue Prism Scheduler?

    A. SQL Server (SQL Authentication)
    B. Availability Group (SQL Authentication)
    C. Blue Prism Server
    D. SQL Server (Windows Authentication)

157. Which of the below option is not a Blue Prism resource pc mode?

    A. Interactive Mode
    B. Resource PC Mode
    C. Command Mode
    D. Robot Mode

158. Which of the following configuration is correct in decision to find if word "prism" is a substring of "Blue Prism"?

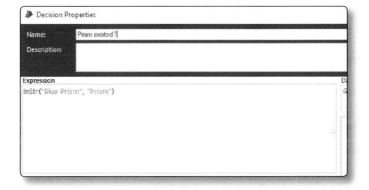

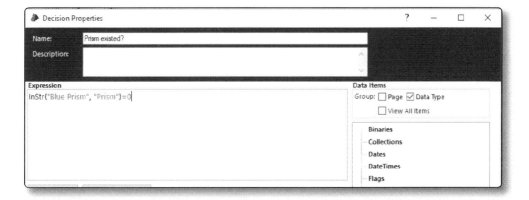

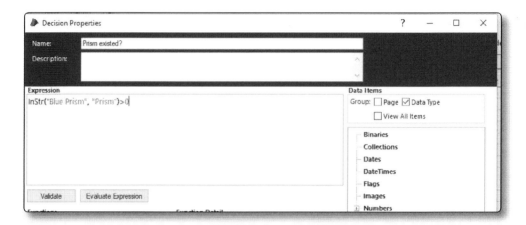

None of the above

159. Which of the below configuration is correct to send enter to a windows application?

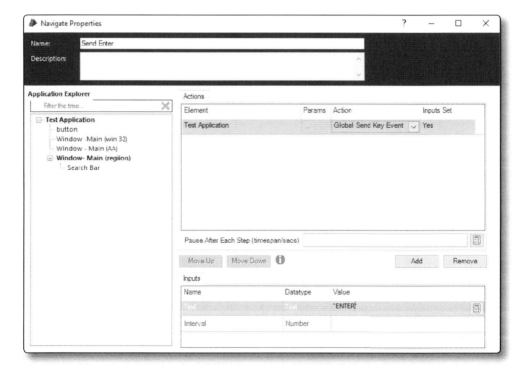

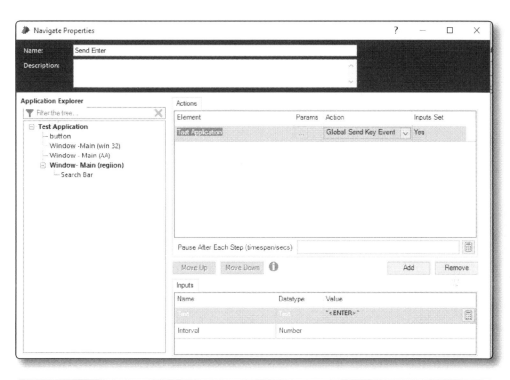

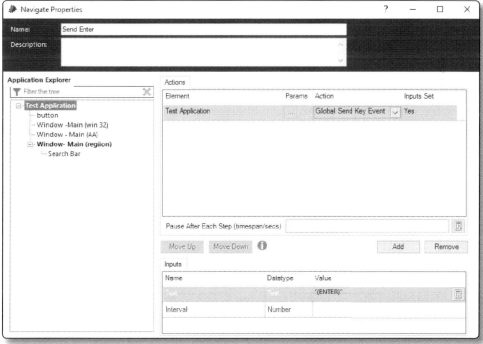

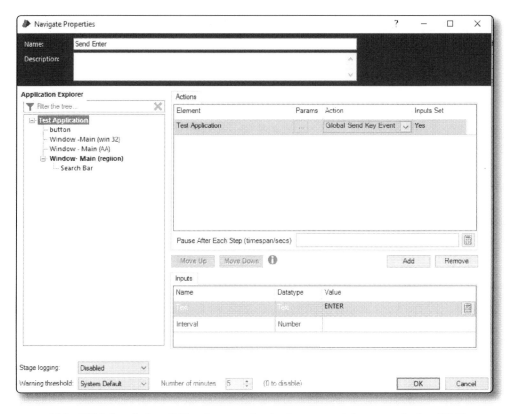

160. Which of the following methods is not used to read the PDF text documents (created using Microsoft Word or Adobe Acrobat)?

A. Using windows clipboard (CTRL+A, CTRL+C, GetClipbaord())

B. Using the Adobe Acrobat API

C. Saving Pdf as XML or word

D. OCR engine

161. Consider the following statements about tagging.

A. Tag can be added to case while adding to the queue using "AddToQueue" action

B. Tag can be added or removed using Work Queue object

C. Tags once added can't be removed or modified

D. Tags will change the priority of work case

Which of the above statement/s is/are correct?

A. 1 and 2

B. 2 and 3

C. 3 and 4

D. 1 and 4

162. Cases in a work queue are tagged with "Business User" or "Normal User". Which of the below configuration is correct to decide the type of the case?

   A. Using TagFilter in GetNextItem Action
   B. Using GetNextItem without tag filter to get itemId, and using getItemData to get the details of case
   C. Using getItemData action to get the value of tag
   D. No action available to know the tag

163. Which of the below property of work queue should be used not to repeat the steps that are already worked for exception case?

   A. Tag
   B. Status
   C. Priority
   D. Key

164. Who should create Solution Design Document as per Blue Prism Life cycle guide lines?

   A. Blue Prism Developer
   B. Blue Prism Technical Architect
   C. Subject Matter Expert
   D. Blue Prism Analyst

165. Which of the below action should be used to read the excel content into Blue Prism collection?

   A. Get Cell Value
   B. Get Worksheet as Collection
   C. Cut
   D. Import CSV

166. Which of the below key board keys should be used to exit the spy mode?

   A. CTRL+ Right Click
   B. CTRL + Left Click
   C. Shift + CTRL
   D. SHIFT+ENTER

167. Which of the below statements best explains the casting in Blue Prism?

   A. Value of one data type is transformed to another data type
   B. Removing the spaces in the value of text data type
   C. Searching the value of data item for certain text
   D. Using number data items in the place of text data item

168. Which of the below stages is used to send global mouse click to the application?

A. Navigate Stage
B. Read Stage
C. Write Stage
D. Action Stage

169. Which of the below functionality of Blue Prism should be used to group the resourcePCs?

A. Active Queues
B. Resource Pools
C. Resource PC
D. Session Manager

170. Which part of Blue Prism is used to add web services?

A. Control Room
B. System Manager
C. Process Studio
D. Application Modeller

171. A change is required to be made in production code. Code has been migrated to lower environments and has been made changes.

Which of the below statements is correct about the importing new release into prod?

A. Processes and objects can't be overwritten in prod
B. Processes and objects can be overwritten
C. Processes and objects should be deleted, and new processes/ objects should be created
D. Processes and objects will be deleted in prod

172. Why break points are used in process flow?

A. To stop the process
B. To restart the process
C. To pause the process
D. To immediate stop the process

173. In a process configuration below error showed.

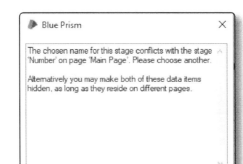

What does this indicate?

A. The data items can't be number type

B. Number Data Item should be hidden

C. There is a stage/data item existing with the name "Number" on page "Main"

D. None of the above

174. In a process, its required to read the table from internet application. Which of the below read stage configuration is correct?

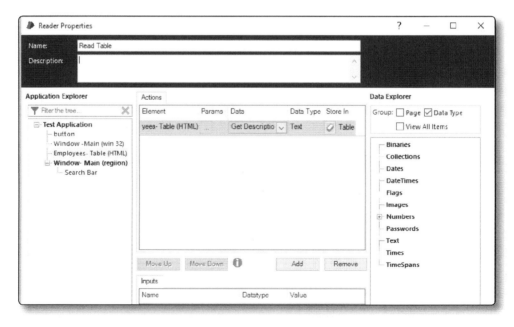

175. A process is configured as below.

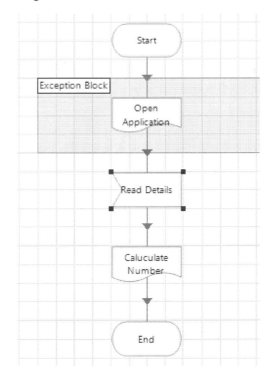

What is the effect of highlighting "Read Details Stage" and selecting "Run to this stage" from right click options?

A. Process skips the execution of all the stages and jumps to read details stage

B. Process executes all the stages and pauses at "Read Details" stage

C. Process skips the execution of "Read Details" stage

D. Process removes the "Read Details" stage

176. Which of the below objects contains "Remove Blank rows" action to remove blank rows from collection?

A. Internal Business object – Collections

B. Internal Business object – Work Queues

C. Utility – Collection Manipulation

D. Utility- General

177. A process page is configured as below.

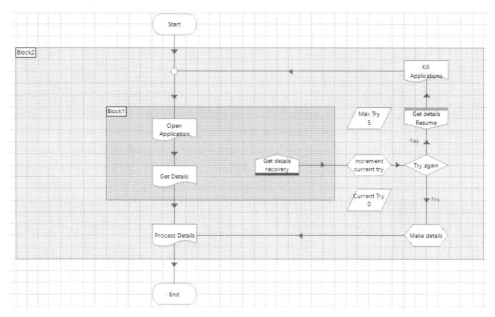

Which of the below statements are correct?

A. Pages executes without exceptions.

B. Block 2 exception block is not having resume and recovery stage. This will throw exception.

C. Block 1 exceptions will be bubbled up to block 2.

D. Blue Prism does not support the nested exception blocks.

178. A page configured as follows.

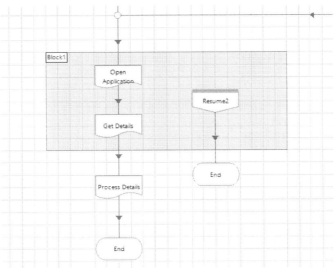

What happens if open applications page throws an exception?

A. Resume stage catches the exception
B. Resume stage rethrows the exception
C. That exception will be bubbled up since block 1 has no recovery stage
D. Process gets terminated

179. A process is configured as below.

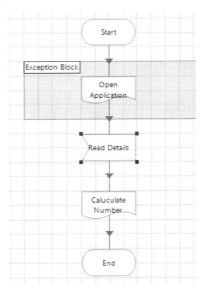

What is the effect of highlighting "Read Details Stage" and selecting "Run to this stage" from right click options?

A. Process skips the execution of all the stages and jumps to read details stage

B. Process executes all the stages and pauses at Read Details stage

C. Process skips the execution of "read details" stage

D. Process removes the "read details" stage

180. Which part of Blue Prism has Application Modeller?

A. Control Room

B. System Manager

C. Process Studio

D. Object Studio

181. Robot encounters below error on execution of "Mark as Completed" action.

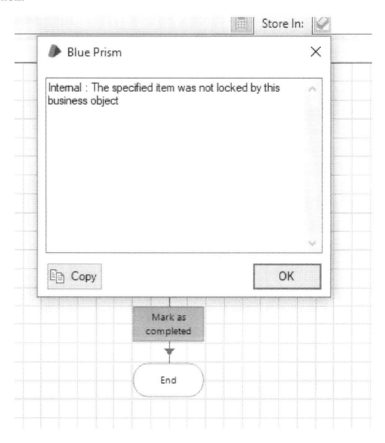

Consider the following scenarios of using Blue Prism Internal Work Queues object that suggest why:

A. "Get Item data" is used to retrieve the queue case data instead of "Get next item action"

B. "Mark as Completed" should always be called along with "Lock action" of work queues object

C. "Unlock Item" action is executed before executing "Mark as Completed"

D. "Update status "should be called before calling "Mark as Completed" action

Which of the above scenarios would cause the error?

A. 1 and 3
B. Only 1
C. 2, 3 and 4
D. Any of the above

182. Which of the below statement is correct regarding session and environmental variables?

A. Session variables are used to share the data among multiple robots
B. Environmental variables and Session variables are interchangeable
C. Session variable can be modified even if the robot is in execution
D. Environmental variables are specific to robot

183. A robot has logic defined in its code as shown below.

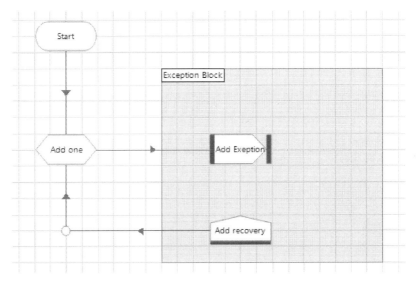

Which of the following option/s is/are valid?

A. Robot goes into infinite loop of the exception

B. Robot does not start the execution

C. Robot gets terminated with the reason defined in the exception block

D. Robot skips the exception block since resume block is not defined in the flow

184. Which of the following stage is present in both process studio and object studio?

A. ☐ Action

B. ◯ Wait

C. ☐ Code

D. ▷ Read

185. How many resume stages can one process have?

A. 0, only objects can have resume stages

B. Any Number

C. 1

D. Number equal to exception blocks

186. Study the following images of wait stage in process flow.

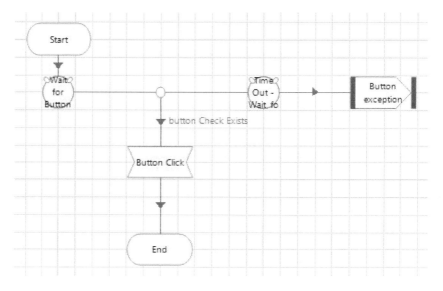

Which of the following statements is correct?

A. The wait stage will wait 5 secs before start looking for button element
B. The wait stage will start looking for button immediately. If the button element is found, the code waits for 5 secs to execute navigate stage
C. The wait stage will start looking for button immediately. If element is found within 5 secs, a system exception will be thrown.
D. The wait stage will start looking for button immediately. If element is not found after 5 secs, a system exception will be thrown.

187. As per Blue Prism best practice guide, what is the best way to manage target application´s credentials in Blue Prism?

A. Should be stored in data item with datatype "Password"
B. Should be stored in Session variable
C. Should be stored in Credential Manager
D. Should be stored as environmental variables

188. In process design flow its necessary to send CTRL+S to the target internet application to save a document. Which of the following is the appropriate usage of native functions of Blue Prism?

A. Global Send Key Events, Input parameter "Text" = "<{CTRL} s>{CTRL}"
B. Global Send Key Events, Input parameter "Text" = "<{CTRL}>s{CTRL}"
C. Global Send keys, Input parameter "Text" = "<{CTRL}s>{CTRL}"
D. Global Send keys, Input parameter "Text" = "<{CTRL}>s{CTRL}"

189. Which of the following documents should be created by the developer?

A. Initial Process Analysis document (IPA) and Process Definition Document (PDD)
B. Solution Design Document (SDD) and Operational Impact Document (OID)
C. Functional Requirements Questionnaire (FRQ) and Operational Impact Document (OID)
D. Process Design Instruction (PDI) and Object Design Instruction (ODI)

190. The work queue "Sample" has many pending items which may be tagged as 1, 2, 3 and 4. What is the correct configuration of Get Next Item to get the case which are tagged as 1 or 4.

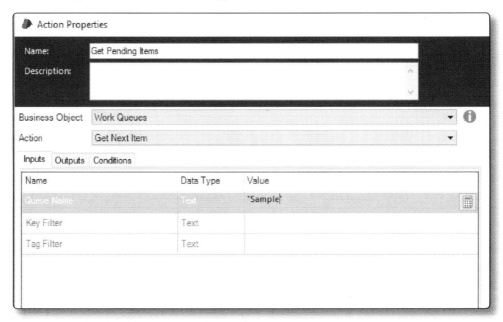

A. Add "1 or 4" in the tag filter parameter
B. Add "1;4" in the tag filter parameter
C. Add "1, 4" in the tag filter parameter
D. Add "-2; -3" in the tag filter parameter

Appendix 2

PROFESSIONAL DEVELOPER EXAM MOCK QUESTIONS

1. Which of the below custom filter should be applied to "created" column in queue view to get the cases that are created between the dates 01-01-2018 and 31-12-2018 (Dates are not inclusive)?

    A. > 01/01/2018, < 01/12/2018
    B. < 01/01/2018, > 01/12/2018
    C. > 01/01/2018 - < 01/12/2018
    D. > 01/01/2018 & < 01/12/2018

2. Which of the below application modes can be used to automate the browse applications?

    - Win32
    - Active Accessibility
    - HTML
    - Region

    A. 3 only
    B. 1 and 3
    C. 1 ,2 and 3
    D. All

3. Which of the following tools can be used to spy the mainframe applications?

    A. Grid Tool
    B. Java Access Bridge
    C. Active Accessibility API
    D. Spy ++

4. Which of the below windows path is correct to enable Java access bridge in windows machine which has java version greater than 7?

A. Start > Control Panel > Ease of Access > Ease of Access Center> Use the computer without a display> Other programs installed

B. Start > Control Panel > Java (32 bits) > Security

C. Start > Control Panel > Java (32 bits)> JAB

D. None of the above

5. Which of the below statements are correct about Blue Prism object layer design?

A. Multiple objects within the object layer provides a more efficient and scalable design

B. Multiple objects within the object layer makes the process run slower

C. One object per application within the object layer makes the process very efficient and scalable

D. Multiple objects within the object layer consumes more memory of the resource PC

6. Which of the below application type should be chosen in application modeller to interact (attach / launch) with Acrobat Pdf application?

A. Windows application

B. Java-based application

C. Mainframe Application

D. Data Base application

7. Which of the below format is used to set up the Login Agent's credential in Credential Manager?

A. Windows Login:ResourcePC

B. Windows Login:{ResourcePC}

C. Windows Login:"ResourcePC"

D. Windows Login:(ResourcePC)

8. Which of the following encryption algorithm is not available in Blue Prism for encrypting credentials or queues?

A. BlowFish

B. AES-256 AesCryptoService

C. AES-256 RijndaelManaged

D. 3DES

9. Which part of the Blue Prism is used to enable the screen capture functionality of exception stage?

    A. Control Room
    B. System Manager
    C. Process Studio
    D. Object Studio

10. What kind of exception will be raised when failed to match an element?

    A. Business Exception
    B. System Exception
    C. Internal Exception
    D. Invalid Element Exception

11. If a process stops cause of unhandled exception. Which of the below status appears in control room for the corresponding session?

    A. Stopped
    B. Immediately Stopped
    C. Terminated
    D. Exception Stopped

12. The work queue "Sample" has many pending items which may be tagged as work type 5, Branch Type 2, Customer Type 10 and Customer Type 2 etc... What is the correct configuration of Get Next Item to get the case which are tagged as worktype5 and customer type 10 but no branch type 10?

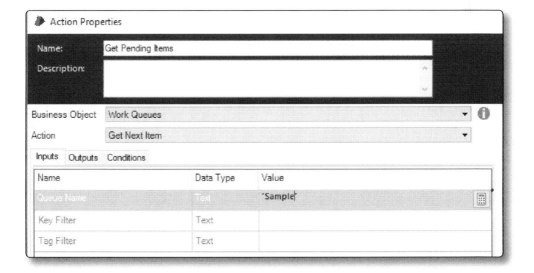

A. Add "+Work Type5; +Customer Type10; -Branch Type10" in the tag filter parameter

B. Add "Work Type5; Customer Type10; Branch Type10" in the tag filter parameter

C. Add "Work Type5, Customer Type10, Branch Type10" in the tag filter parameter

D. Add "-Work Type5; -Customer Type10; +Branch Type10" in the tag filter parameter

13. Which of the below statement is correct about using tags to filter the work queues?

A. An asterisk character is used to search for 'any other characters', and a question mark character is used to search for 'any single character' in a tag

B. An asterisk character is used to search for 'any single character', and a question mark character is used to search for 'any other characters' in a tag

C. Blue prism work queues get next item action does not support tags to be used for filtering

D. None of the above

14. Which of the below statements is correct about a work queue case that has "Differed" status?

A. The case has been chosen to process on deferred date

B. The case has been chosen to be deleted manually

C. The case will be deleted once Blue prism is closed

D. The case has been successfully worked

15. Which of the below is the correct configuration "Tag Filter" property of Get Next Item to get the case which has literal asterisks in its tag?

A. "*"

B. "/*"

C. "**"

D. "+*"

16. Which of the following statements is correct about work queue case status?

    A. Work Queue case status can be changed multiple times
    B. Work Queue status can only be set at the time of adding it to queue
    C. Work Queue status can be deleted
    D. None of the above

17. Which of the following OCR engine is used by Blue Prism for surface automation?

    A. Google Colud Vision
    B. IBM Data Cap
    C. Abbyy SDK
    D. Teserract

18. Which of the below action of work queue object can be used to set the priority after case has already been added to queue?

    A. Set Priority
    B. Update Priority
    C. Modify Priority
    D. None

19. Which of the below approach is used by Blue Prism work queues to handle the work cases?

    A. First in, Last Out (FILO)
    B. First in, First Out (FIFO)
    C. Today first
    D. Future day first

20. Which of the below statement is correct about getting next case item from queue when there are cases with different priorities?

    A. Get Next Item selects items in order of lowest priority number first
    B. Get Next Item selects items in order of highest priority number first
    C. Get Next Item selects items in order of negative priority number first
    D. Get Next Item selects items in order of decimal priority number first

21. Which part of blue prism should be used to change the encryption scheme or disable encryption of work queue?

   A. Control Room
   B. System Manager
   C. Process Studio
   D. Object Studio

22. What type of exceptions can be reworked?

   A. System Exceptions
   B. Business Exceptions
   C. Invalid Input Exceptions
   D. No exception should be reworked

23. A process has multiple steps to be processed and there should be one-week time gap between any two steps. Which of the below work queue configuration model best suits if developer wants to consume one license for the process?

   A. Dividing the work of process between two robots and running them on two different machines
   B. Using a single work queue and deferring the case item for a week
   C. Diving the work between Blue Prism robot and humans
   D. Blue Prism cannot automate processes which are multipart

24. Study the below scenario.

   A business process is triggered by an email containing hundreds of items to work in its body. Multiple email will be received to work throughout the day. A Work Queue item is created for each item in the email. When all the items in email body have been worked, an email needs to be sent with details specific to the items on that email.

   Consider the following configurations of work queues?

   A. A new work queue should be created manually for every email
   B. A case item can be tagged by name and sender of the email and retrieved by using same value in get next item action
   C. Different mail boxes should be employed to receive the mails and to trigger multiple robots with different work queues
   D. Blue Prism can't automate this scenario

25. An action called "Attach (or Launch)" fails with following exception.

"Internal: failed to perform step 1 in navigate stage 'Attach' on page 'attach (or launch)' – Target application could not be identified"

What might have caused the above exception?

A. Navigate stage should not be used to attach to the application
B. More than one element found in target application with same foot print
C. Target application has not been launched or is not running
D. Its Blue Prism product's internal exception

26. Which of the below is not work queue design methodology?

A. Multi-Part Processes – Deferring and Multiple Queues
B. Parent/Child Relationships in queues
C. Workflow Systems to populate work queues
D. Manual creation of work case items

27. A subpage of a process has been configured to have two navigate stages. One navigate stage is to launch the application and followed by another navigate stage to attach to the application.

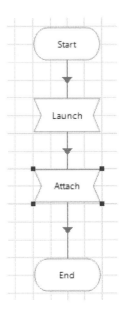

Consider the following statements about the execution of the page.

A. Page gets executed successfully

B. Attach should be configured before Launch

C. Attach navigate stage throws exception

D. Launch Navigate stage throws exception

28. A page is configured to have two recover stages without using any exception block.

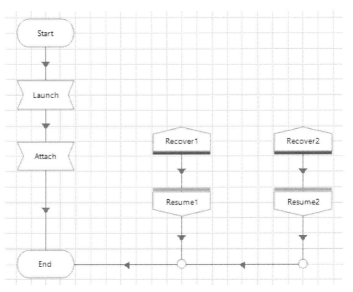

What problem is there in the page design?

A. A page should not have two recover stages

B. A page should not have two resume stages

C. Exception Block should be used in a page

D. Multiple recover or resume stages in a page is redundant

29. A page is configured to have two recover stages without using any exception block.

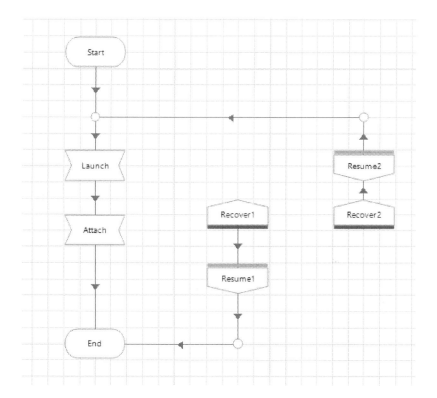

If an exception happens at Launch navigate stage, which recover path would be taken?

A. Page will be executed successfully by takin recover1 path

B. Page will go to infinite loop by taking recover2 path

C. Page will throw error since there is no Exception Block

D. None of the above

30. Which of the below is not internal exception?

A. Not Connected
B. Already connected to an application
C. Decision did not result in a yes/no answer
D. Validation exception

31. Where will exception retry logic implemented in a process design?

A. Sub Pages
B. Business Object
C. Main Page
D. None

32. Which of the below stage is used to isolate the exception on a page?

A. Action Stage
B. Recover Stage
C. Resume Stage
D. Exception Block Stage

33. Which of the below expression in the Retry? decision stage is correct to have the robot to retry in case of system and internal exceptions?

A. [RetryCount]<[RetryLimit]AND(Lower(ExceptionType())="system exception" OR Lower(ExceptionType())="internal")
B. [RetryCount]>[RetryLimit]AND(Lower(ExceptionType())="system exception" OR Lower(ExceptionType())="internal")
C. [Retry Count] < [Retry Limit] AND (Lower(ExceptionType())<>"system exception" OR Lower(ExceptionType())="internal")
D. [RetryCount]<[RetryLimit]AND(Lower(ExceptionType())="system exception" OR Lower(ExceptionType())<>"internal")

34. Study the below configuration.

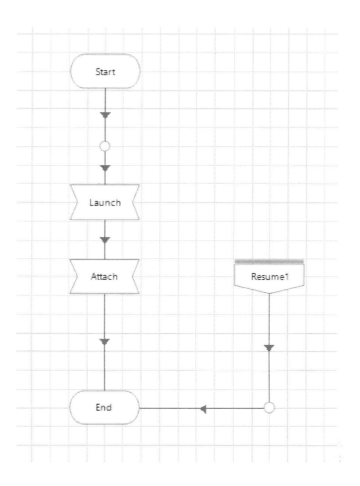

What problem is there in the page design?

A. Resume stage should not be connected to end stage
B. Anchor stage should not be connected from start stage
C. Missing recover stage on the page
D. No problem

35. A page has been configured as shown in the below diagram.

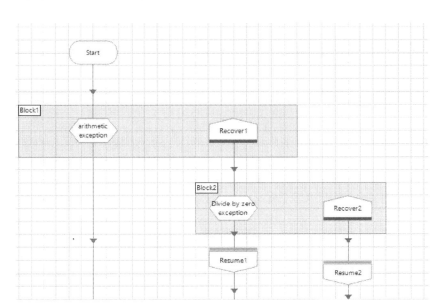

What happen if page is executed?

A. Recover2 stage path will be executed
B. Exception block is allowed in recover mode
C. Process gets terminated with divide by zero exception
D. Process gets terminated with arithmetic exception

36. Which module of Blue Prism is used to configure Queue Item Retries?

A. Control Room
B. Process Studio
C. Dash Board
D. System Manager

37. In a process execution below exception was encountered

"Internal: stack imbalance has reached".

What might have caused this exception?

A. The process or business object was in Exception mode and a new exception is thrown
B. End stage was executed while process Is in recover mode
C. The process has 100 errors
D. Recover stage was not implemented on the any page

38. A page has been configured as shown in the below diagram.

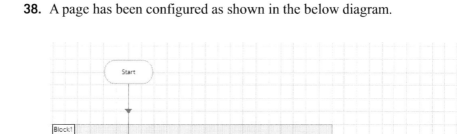

Consider the following statements.

A. Arithmetic exception will be caught by Recover1 stage
B. Divide by zero exception will be caught by Recover2 stage
C. Recove1 stage has no effect on arithmetic exception
D. Recover2 stage has no effect on arithmetic exception

39. A page has been configured as below.

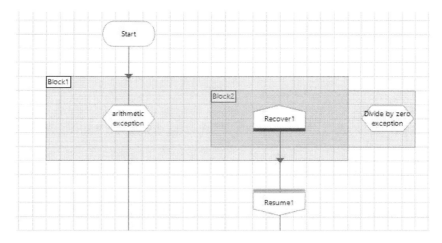

What happens on the execution of the page?

A. Recover1 path will be executed

B. Process gets terminated as exception blocks are overlapping

C. Process does not start there is link attached to dived by zero exception stage

D. None of the above

40. A process was terminated with below error.

What might have caused the error?

A. Properties of an unhandled exception stage are left blank

B. Its Blue Prism internal code bug

C. Process terminated with internal exception

D. Preserve check was not used properly

41. A Work Queue case was marked as exception having no exception details. Consider the below scenarios.

A. Properties of an unhandled exception stage are left blank

B. Its Blue Prism internal code bug

C. Process terminated with internal exception

D. Preserve check was not used properly

42. Multiple developers need to work on a process which involves multiple applications.

Which of the below statement is true for this scenario?

A. A design having multiple objects within the object layer

B. Work Shifts to access the process and objects

C. Divide the process into various processes based on applications

D. Having all the developers working using one user Id

43. Which of the below object layer design is recommended by Blue Prism?

    A. One business object for every screen of the application

    B. One business object for every sub task of the process

    C. One business object for entire process

    D. None of the above

44. A page in a business object is configured as below.

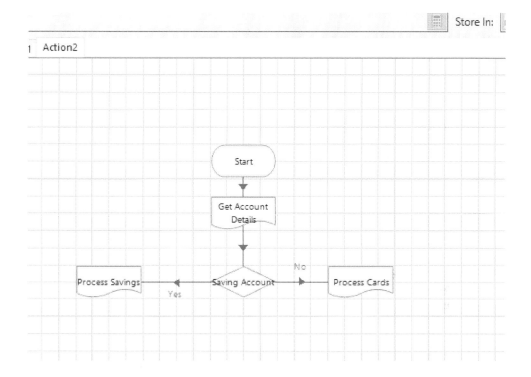

What problem has the object page design?

    A. Wait stage should be implemented in every action

    B. Action stage should be used to call process saving and process cards pages

    C. Business decisions should not happen in objects

    D. No issues in the design

45. Which of the below statement explains the difference between Request Stop and Immediate Stop?

    A. "Request stop" ends the process execution slowly but "Immediate Stop" ends execution immediately

B. "Request stop" ends the process execution which are running on resource PC and "Immediate Stop" stops the processes that are on interactive client machine

C. "Request Stop" has no effect if IsStopRequested () function check is not implemented in process and "Immediate Stop" stops the processes irrespective of the check

D. No difference

46. How many tags can one Blue Prism queue case have?

A. 1

B. 2

C. 0

D. No limit

47. Which part of the blue prism is used to expose processes or objects as Web Services?

A. Control Room

B. Process Studio

C. Dash Board

D. System Manager

48. Which of the below URL is used to confirm the web services that are exposed from Blue Prism?

A. http://[machinename]:[Blue Prismport]/ws/

B. http://[machinename]/ws/

C. http://[machinename]:[port]/[process Name]

D. http://[machinename]:[port]/ws/[ObjectName]

49. Which of the below requirement is obligatory to expose Blue Prism's process or object as webservice?

A. Process or object name should contain only alphanumeric characters

B. Process or object should use code stage

C. Configuration of webservice should be done in process or object with code stage

D. No requirement to expose blue prism components as web services

50. How the external web services that are added to blue prism will be available in process studio?

A. Processes

B. Business Objects

C. Actions

D. Pages

51. Which of the below command line (automate switch) is used to register a web service?

A. /regwebservice
B. /addwebservice
C. /exposewebservice
D. /modwebservice

52. What is WSDL?

A. Web Service Description Language
B. Web Service Definition Language
C. Web Service Design Language
D. Web Service Direct Language

53. Which of the below is the equivalent .NET data type of flag data type of Blue Prism?

A. Boolean
B. Char
C. String
D. Bit

54. Which of the below is not access authentication to consume external webservices in blue prism?

A. IP based authentication
B. Certificate based authentication
C. Username and password as part of the HTTP header
D. WS-Security authentication

55. Which of the below stage is used to interfacing with a COM (Component object models) object in a Microsoft Windows environment?

A. Code Stage
B. Action Stage
C. Page Stage
D. Sub Process Stage

56. Which of the below data type of the blue prism is used to map the complex data types (list, arrays) of external web services?

A. Numbers
B. Collections
C. Strings
D. List

57. There are 5 processes exposed as web service. How many licenses are required to connect to 3 exposed processes simultaneously?

A. 5

B. 8

C. 3

D. 1

58. Three business objects with run mode back ground are exposed as web services. How many sessions are created in a resource machine for connecting to three Business Object using auto-initialization concurrently?

A. 0

B. 1

C. 3

D. Equal number of calls

59. Three business objects with run mode "Exclusive" are exposed as web services. How many resourcePCs are required for connecting to three Business Object using auto-initialization concurrently?

A. 0

B. 1

C. 3

D. Equal number of calls

60. How many sessions are created in a resource machine for connecting to a Business Object using auto-initialization?

A. 0

B. 1

C. Number of business objects exposed

D. Number of calls to connect

61. Three business objects with run mode "Exclusive" are exposed as web services. How many licenses are required for connecting to three Business Object using auto-initialization concurrently?

A. 0

B. 1

C. 3

D. Equal number of calls

62. How many sessions are created for connecting to a Business Object using manual-initialization?

   A. 0

   B. 1

   C. Equal number of service calls

   D. None of the above

63. How many initialization methods are available to connect to Business Object which is exposed as web service?

   A. 0

   B. 1

   C. 2

   D. Many

64. Which of the below run mode is used to run multiple sessions in a single resource machine?

   A. Fore ground

   B. Exclusive

   C. Back ground

   D. None

65. Machine1 is currently executing a process, Process A, in Exclusive run mode. In quick succession it receives 5 web service requests targeted at another Process B which is of foreground.

Consider the following outcomes

   A. Execution of Process A will be stopped to allocate machine to process B

   B. 5 sessions will be created on machine 1

   C. 6 sessions will be created on macine1

   D. 5 web service calls will be rejected to make session

66. Machine1 is currently executing a process, Process A, in Foreground run mode. In quick succession it receives 5 web service requests targeted at another Process B which is of foreground.

Consider the following outcomes

   A. Execution of Process A will be stopped to allocate machine to process B

   B. 5 sessions will be created on machine 1

   C. 6 sessions will be created on macine1

   D. 5 web service calls will be rejected to make session

67. Which of the below tool can be used to generate Auto-Generate Code of external webservices?

A. wsdl.exe
B. SOAP.exe
C. SOAPUI.exe
D. Vs.exe

68. How many initialization methods are available for consuming process-based web service?

A. 0
B. 1
C. 2
D. 3

69. Which of the below authentication method is used to access Blue Prism web services?

A. HTTP authentication
B. WS-Security
C. Certificate based authentication
D. IP Based authentication

70. Which of the below stage is used to call the methods of external web services?

A. Action Stage
B. Page Stage
C. Sub Process Stage
D. Calculation Stage

71. A process is designed to work on second tab of the internet explorer. Which of the below configuration of navigate stage is correct to attach to second tab?

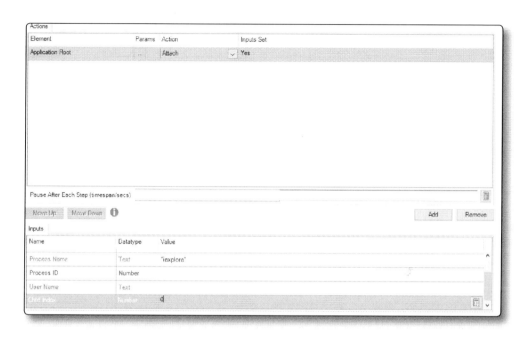

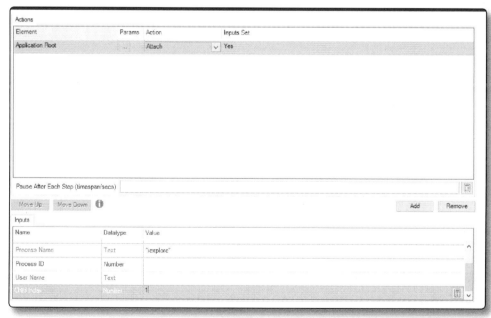

72. When a developer trying to attach to the internet explorer with multiple tabs, he /she finds multiple processes running with name "iexplorer" in task manager.

    Which of the below statement explain this scenario?

    A. Web application is designed to create multiple Internet explorer processes
    B. Blue Prism created multiple sessions of Internet Explorer
    C. Internet explorer creates a separate process for each tab
    D. None of the above

73. Which of the below native action is used to get the values from HTML table in Read Stage?

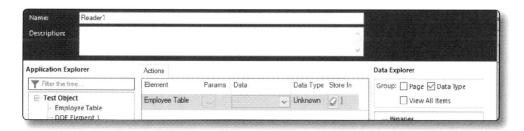

    A. Get Table
    B. Get Current Value
    C. Get Description
    D. Get Name

74. Which of the following application modeller element should be used to make inter process communication under Microsoft Windows with Blue Prism?

    A. DDE element
    B. HTML elements
    C. AA elements
    D. Win32 elements

75. In an action its required to wait for current page to be fully loaded. Below are the properties of the wait stage.

Which of the below condition should be used to wait till page is loaded?

A. Document Loaded

B. Parent Document Loaded

C. Check Page Exist

D. Check Exist

76. In an action its required to wait for a page and its child frames are to be fully loaded. Below are the properties of the wait stage of the action.

Which of the below condition should be used to wait till page is loaded?

A. Document Loaded

B. Parent Document Loaded

C. Check Page Exist

D. Check Exist

77. Which of the below is not the HTML attribute of application modeller?

A. Parent URL

B. Path

C. Style

D. Class Name

78. To automate Silverlight applications easily which of the below property needs to be set to false?

A. The Windowless property

B. Active Accessibility property

C. Windows32 property

D. None

79. A web application has java script function to update details on the screen. Navigate stage properties are as follows.

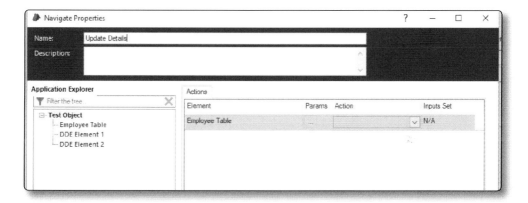

Which of the below action should be used in navigate stage to call the function?

A. Insert JavaScript Fragment

B. Invoke JavaScript

C. Call JavaScript

D. Execute JavaScript

80. Which of the below mode should be used to identify ActiveX components within target browser application?

A. Active Accessibility (AA) mode

B. Win32 Mode

C. HTML mode

D. Surface Automation

81. Which of the below parameter is used by Blue Prism to start or attach to a mainframe application?

A. Session Identifier

B. Mainframe Vendor

C. Server Name

D. Title

82. A process which work on main frame application encountered a below error on launch.

"Unable to load DLL 'HLLAPI32.DLL': The specified module could not be found"

What does the error indicate?

A. Mainframe is not installed on the machine
B. New mainframe which is not listed in Blue Prism options
C. Mainframe installation directory is not added to Windows PATH environment variable
D. Resource PC can't not be used to run mainframe applications

83. A navigate stage has been configured t o s end t he k eys 'u' 's' 'e' 'r' 'ENTER' to a mainframe application?

Below are the properties of navigate stage.

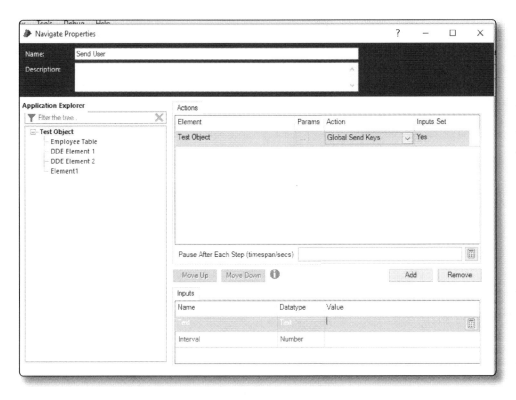

Which of the below is correct value of the property "Text" of the navigate stage?

A. user{enter}

B. user<enter>

C. user"enter"

D. None of the above

84. Which version of java should be installed to integrate with target system with mode "Embedded"?

    A. 64 bit

    B. 32 bit

    C. Either of them

    D. None

85. Which of the below application manager mode should be used to integrate with applications which use 64-bit java?

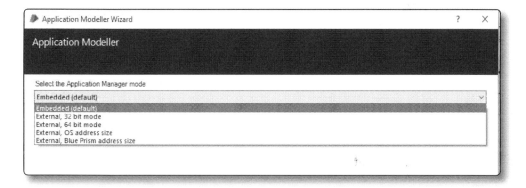

    A. Embedded (default)

    B. External ,32 bit

    C. External,64 bit

    D. External, OS address size

86. Which of the below functionality of application modeller scans the target application design if application prevents using any spying mode?

    A. Application Navigator

    B. DDE elements

    C. HTC components

    D. Diagnostics

87. Which of the below option should be used in application modeller wizard to ignore all invisible elements in java applications?

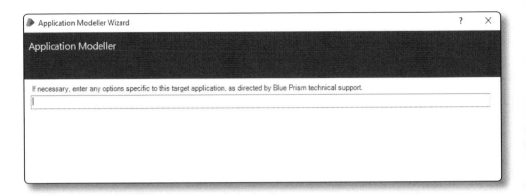

A. Descendtree

B. Ignorenotshowing

C. Ancestorcount

D. NotShowing

88. Which of the below option should be used in application modeller wizard to search the entire Application Model Tree for elements within the target Java application?

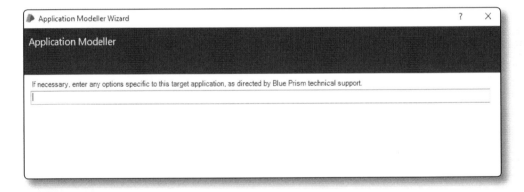

A. Descendtree

B. Ignorenotshowing

C. Ancestorcount

D. NotShowing

89. Which of the below technique should be used to read the text from the scanned images in PDF document?

A. OCR

B. String Manipulations

C. Regions

D. Conversion of PDF to Word

90. Which of the below program should be used to interact with PDF documents?

A. Google Chorome

B. Internet Explorer

C. Acrobat PDF Reader

D. Microsoft word

91. Which of the below OCR engine is used by Blue Prism to read images?

A. Tessetact

B. Google cloud vision

C. Abbyy fine reader

D. OCR.Space

92. Which of the below security policy should be implemented in resource PC for Login Agent?

A. Do not require CTRL + ALT + DEL

B. Do not require wallpaper

C. Lock screen should be enabled

D. None of the above

93. Which of the below permissions a user should have to access the credentials in Blue Prism?

A. Security - Manage Credentials

B. Processes - Configure Credentials

C. Objects - Configure Credentials

D. Control Room

94. Which of the below blue prism's functionality should be used to manage sensitive information?

A. Work Queue

B. Encryption

C. Credential Manager

D. Data Base

95. Study the below configuration of credential.

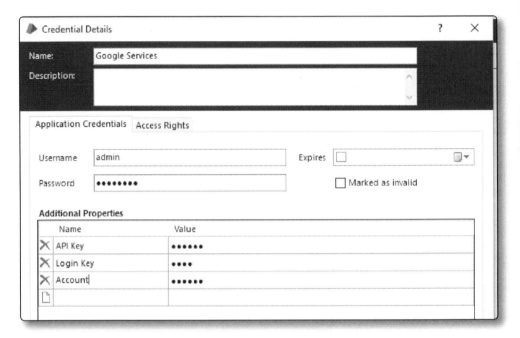

Which of the below action of credentials Business object should be used to retrieve the value of login Key?

A. Read Property
B. List Property
C. Retrieve Property
D. Get Property

96. Which of the below Blue Prism module should be used to create custom calendar?

A. Control Room
B. System Manager
C. Process Studio
D. Object Studio

97. Which of the below configuration should be used to register machines of various domains as resourcePCs?

A. Register using machine (short) name, communicate using FQDN
B. Register and communicate using machine short name
C. Register and communicate using the Operating Unit of machines

  D. None of the above

98. Which of the below spying mode is used in surface automation?

  A. Active Accessibility (AA) mode
  B. Win32 Mode
  C. HTML mode
  D. Region Mode

99. Which of the below automation method should be used to automate applications that are hosted in Citrix?

  A. Java Automation Techniques
  B. Browser Automation Techniques
  C. Surface Automation Techniques
  D. Citrix Automation

100. Which of the below is not an action of reader stage action of regions?

  A. Read Text
  B. Read Image
  C. Recognise Text
  D. Recognise Image

101. Which of the below utility is used for surface automation?

  A. Utility – General
  B. Utility- Image Manipulation
  C. Utility – Surface Automation
  D. Utility – Citrix

102. Which of the below native function of Blue Prism is used to read the text using OCR technique from Images?

  A. Read Text with OCR
  B. Read Text
  C. Read Text (OCR)
  D. OCR

103. Which of the below native function of Blue Prism is used to read the text using invasive technique from Images?

  A. Read Text with OCR
  B. Read Text
  C. Read Text (OCR)
  D. OCR

104. Which of the below path should be used to install tesseract language files in Blue Prism resource PC?

A. C:\Program Files\Blue Prism Limited\Blue Prism Automate\Tesseract\ tessdata

B. C:\Program Files\Blue Prism Limited\Blue Prism Automate\Tesseract\ tessdata\languages

C. C:\Program Files\Blue Prism Limited\Blue Prism Automate\Tesseract\

D. C:\Program Files\Blue Prism Limited\Blue Prism Automate\Tesseract\ Languages

105. In a process it's required to use tesseract for text extraction, which of the below clarity resolution is minimum required?

A. 300 dots-per-inch

B. 600 dots-per-inch

C. 800 dots-per-inch

D. 1200 dots-per-inch

Appendix 3

DEVELOPER EXAM ANSWERS

Question: 1

ANSWER: **C**

▶ Option A is incorrect because Application Modeller is used to spy the elements and identify the spied elements during application navigation.

▶ Option B is incorrect because Object studio is used to create actions to interact with the target application using the elements which are spied by application modeller.

▶ Option C is correct because Process studio is right place to configure business logic and rules. Configuring logic in Process Studio gives the more control for the change management.

▶ Option D is incorrect because control room is used to perform daily executions, schedules, view queues etc.

Question: 2

ANSWER: **C**

▶ Option A is incorrect because ToDate() function can't interpret the text which is not separated by – or / for making a date. ToDate() function can only convert strings that are divided by – or / to date.

▶ Option B is incorrect because "23032018" is passed as argument to the ToDate() function, which throws the below error in execution.

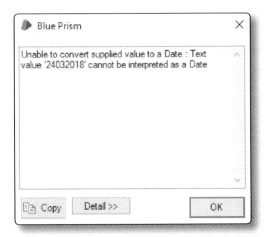

▶ Option C is correct because ToDate () function can only convert strings that are divided by – or / to date. 1 and 3 options have string separated by – or /.

▶ Option D is incorrect cause of input parameter "24;03;2018" to the ToDate () function.

Question: 3

ANSWER: B

▶ Option A is not correct because execution of Open Application does not go into infinite loop since no page is chosen in properties.

▶ Option B is correct because execution of Open Application throws the below error.

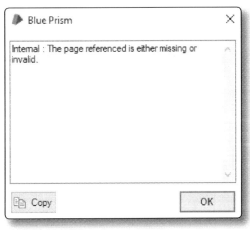

▶ Option C is incorrect because Blue Prism always ignores the compiler errors except code compilation errors.

▶ Option D is incorrect because Option B is correct.

Question: 4

ANSWER: **B**

▶ Option A is incorrect because elements spied using Active Accessibility mode does not offer activate application action.

▶ Option B is correct because win 32`s attribute "Windows Text" is used to find the foreground window later Blue Prism make a call to the operating system to identify the Windows process in control of the foreground window.

▶ Option C is incorrect because region spying mode works by searching region´s stored images at run time.

▶ Option D is incorrect because HTML spying mode work by searching elements in HTML layout.

Question: 5

ANSWER: **A**

▶ Option A is correct because exception reason "Automatically set exception at clean up" is set up by Blue Prism if queue case is not declared as completed or exception. This could occur when machine restarts when process is in execution, process gets terminated before declaring previous item or takes another case with our declaring the previous case.

▶ Option B is incorrect because resume stage nullifies the recovery mode of the execution of the process. Resume mode does not configure the exception reason of the work queue cases.

▶ Option C is incorrect because if no exception block is mentioned in code, any exception can terminate the process. If a process gets terminated with unhandled exception, error message of the unhandled exception would be stored as exception reason of the case.

▶ Option D is incorrect because Developer should use the exception reason which would help the business people to understand the execution of case.

Question: 6

ANSWER: **B**

▶ Option A is not correct because control room is used to monitoring the daily execution, queue status and schedules.

▶ Option B is correct because Environmental variables, Queues, credentials, resource pools and calendars are should be created in system Manager.

▶ Option C is incorrect because Process studio is used to create the process containing business logic and business rules.

▶ Option d is incorrect because object studio is used to spy the elements of the target application and to create actions to interact with the application.

Question: 7

ANSWER: **A**

▶ Option A is Correct to add days to any date, Blue Prism native date functions should be used.

▶ Option B is incorrect cause of the incorrect syntax, Blue Prism can't not interpret ":" as delimiter.

▶ Option C is incorrect because "+" operator cannot be applied to date time parameters.

▶ Option D is incorrect because Blue Prism does not natively have Tomorrow () function.

Question: 8

ANSWER: **D**

▶ Option A is not correct because a case should never be deleted from the queue. Queue is central system that saves the robot load. This data of the queue should be used to review with the business people.

▶ Option B is not correct because process can't be run if the system is shutdown.

▶ Option C is incorrect cause the if process encounters a case which is not defined in the scope, it should be marked as business exception so that business people would take for manual processing.

▶ Option D is correct because if system does not respond to the robot, robot should mark it as system exception and restart the machine before picking up the next item from queue.

Question: 9

ANSWER: **C**

▶ Option A is incorrect because step through the page would Execute the page.

▶ Option B is incorrect because step over would execute the page, but debug control would not display the execution of steps in page "Open Application".

▶ Option C is correct because highlighting "Read Details" stage and selecting "Set Next Stage" makes the process skip the execution of "Open Application" page.

▶ Option D is incorrect because it's possible to skip the execution of the stages in process.

Question: 10

ANSWER: **C**

▶ Option A is incorrect because exception block has an exception bock defined in it., and no inbound link is defined to raise the exception.

▶ Option B is incorrect because exception has been rethrown after using resume stage. Resume stage nullifies the exception, hence rethrowing is not possible after executing resume. Use of "preserve exception "after resume would throw unhandled exception.

▶ Option C is correct because the 'Preserve' checkbox is only applicable when in Recovery Mode.

▶ Option D is incorrect because exception block has resume defined in it. Resume stage should always be followed by recover stage. Resume stage alone does not server any purpose in process flow.

Question: 11

ANSWER: C

▶ Option A is not correct because to make changes to configuration environmental variables are used.

▶ Option B is not correct because session variables are used to control the execution flow of the running process.

▶ Option C is correct that statistic variables are used to store the content of data item in data base for reporting purposes.

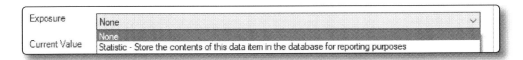

▶ Option D is incorrect because Blue Prism has static variables available in it.

Question: 12

ANSWER: D

▶ Option A is incorrect because page can only use one recover stage unless blocks are used. Any exception occurred on this page would be caught by the recovery stage on that page.

▶ Option B is incorrect because exceptions can be handled anywhere in the process. There are no restrictions to use exception handling in a process.

▶ Option C is incorrect because a Page can have multiple blocks and multiple recovery stages. Example is give below.

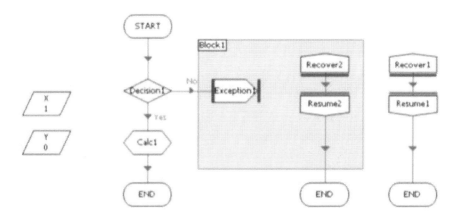

▶ Option D is correct because blocks should not overlap, and blocks cannot be nested.

Question: 13

ANSWER: D

▶ Option A is incorrect because value data items initial value is 500. After execution 10000, 100 gets added to the 500.

▶ Option B is incorrect because initial value 500 is also gets added to 10000, and 100.

▶ Option C is incorrect because "+" operation on number data items adds all the number values.

▶ Option D is correct because 10000+100+500 = 10600.

Question: 14

ANSWER: A

▶ Option A is correct because every exception increases the correct count data item. Decision stage check if the value of "Current count" data item is less than or equal to "max count" to make decision. Decision stage decides to retry when current count item is equal to max count.

▶ Option B is incorrect because initial value of the "max count" is greater than the value of "current count", hence decision stage takes the path to rethrow the exception first time.

▶ Option C is incorrect because "max count" data item value is never less than the "current count" data item value.

▶ Option D is incorrect because decision stage takes rethrow path after trying two times.

Question: 15

ANSWER: **C**

▶ Option A is incorrect because Blue Prism is not used for transfer data from on system to another system.

▶ Option B is incorrect because Blue Prism is not used to link the applications.

▶ Option C is correct because Blue Prism is a software to create digital workforce which enables organizations like yours to automate existing user actions.

▶ Option D is incorrect because Blue Prism is used to automate the use tasks.

Question: 16

ANSWER: **C**

▶ Option A is incorrect because if exposure of the data items is none, it can't be accessed from another page. This kind of variables are called local variables.

▶ Option B is not correct because to make changes to configuration environmental variables are used.

▶ Option C is correct because session variables are used to control the execution flow of the running process. In this context based on the value of "Stop ASAP" data item, process can stop the execution instead of taking a next pending case from queue.

▶ Option D Is incorrect because static is used to save the value of the data item in data base for reporting purposes.

Question: 17

ANSWER: **B**

> Option A is incorrect because tags of work queue are used to filter the pending item based on tag filter criteria.

> Option B is correct because the status is a useful way of recording how far through your process a Work Queue item has been worked. Status can help to do the following things:

- See from the Queue Management screen the progress of an item

- If an item is to be re-worked following an exception the Status could be used to skip steps in the process flow that have already been completed for that item

> Option C is incorrect because priority is used to set the priority. Get Next Item function high priority case items from work queue.

> Option D is incorrect because attempt parameter is used to count the number of retries of the work case in case of system exceptions.

Question: 18

ANSWER: **C**

> Option A is incorrect because wait stage has native condition to check the window attribute.

> Option B is incorrect because wait stage has native condition to check AA attributes.

> Option C is correct because wait stage does not have condition to check region attributes.

> Option D is correct because wait stage has native condition to check HTML attributes.

Question: 19

ANSWER: **D**

▶ Option A is incorrect because step button would step into the "open Application" and will pause on start stage of the page.

▶ Option B is incorrect because step over would execute the page, but debug control would not display the execution of steps in page "Open Application".

▶ Option C is incorrect because Highlight "Read Details" stage and select "Set Next Stage" makes the process skip the execution of "Open Application" page.

▶ Option D is correct because Step Out continues running until the flow moves out of the current page/sub-process back to the stage which called the current page/sub-process.

Question: 20

ANSWER: **A**

▶ Option A is correct because key of the work queue is visible in control room. If this key is sensitive data like credit card number, bank account number, SSN number, key should be encrypted.

▶ Option B is incorrect because if Key Name parameter is not configured, key filter in Get Next Item can't be used to pick the items based on key value.

▶ Option C is incorrect because priority of the case is to prioritize the processing of the cases.

▶ Option D is incorrect because Blue Prism work queues does not encrypt the work queues if it's not configured explicitly in Queue configuration of system tag.

Question: 21

ANSWER: **B**

▶ Option A is not correct because .

- scenario 1: Process can be configured to use the objects with different run modes. If a process uses objects with multiple run modes, it does not impact its execution from control room.

- Scenario 2: Every process created can be run on another machine using control room.

▶ Option B is correct because scenario 3: if a process is not published, it will not be listed in control room. Publishing can be done as in the below image.

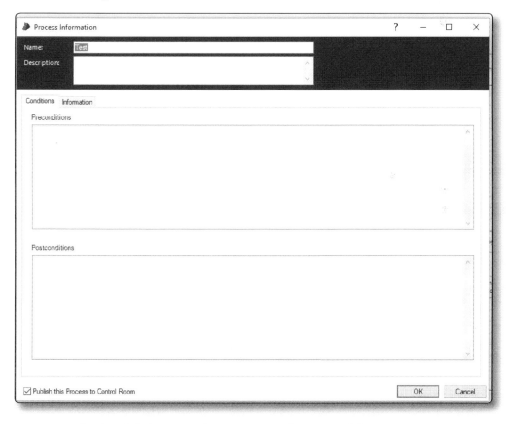

▶ Option C is incorrect because scenario 1,2 are false.

▶ Option D is incorrect because scenarios 1, 2 and 4 do not impact the process visibility in the control room.

Question: 22

ANSWER: **C**

▶ Option A is incorrect because a page can have more than one end stage. A page should at least have one end stage.

▶ Option B is incorrect because a page can have more than two end stages. A page should at least have one end stage.

▶ Option C is correct because page can have multiple end stages. Process can take multiple paths reaching various end points.

▶ Option D is incorrect because a page should at least have one end stage.

Question: 23

ANSWER: **D**

Blue Prism system manager provide all the functionalities that are mentioned in the options. Below image depicts the options in system manager.

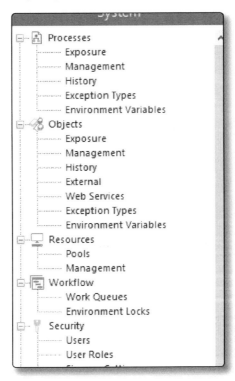

Question: 24

ANSWER: **A**

> ▶ Option A is correct because the 'unable to match with query terms' message is Application Modeller's way of telling you it cannot find the element. Essentially it is saying 'I can't see the element that you referenced anymore'.

> ▶ Option B is incorrect because if "Input User Credentials" stage could find multiple elements conflicting with the element referenced in "Input User Credentials" stage, it would show below error.

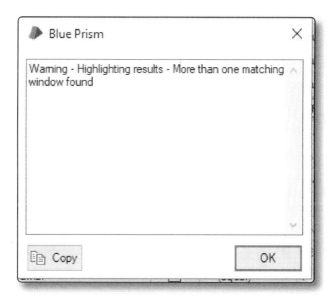

> ▶ Option C is incorrect because "Input User Credentials" is read stage and can't be used to attach to the application.

> ▶ Option D is incorrect because "Input User Credentials" is a stage used to input credentials in an application.

Question: 25

ANSWER: **B**

> ▶ Option A is incorrect case that start stage does not accept inbound link, but it does accept out bound link.

▶ Option B is correct because end stage does accept the inbound link. But does not accept the outbound link.

▶ Option C is incorrect because navigate stage does accept inbound and outbound links.

▶ Option D is incorrect because Alert stage does accept inbound and outbound links.

Question: 26

ANSWER: **B**

▶ Option A is incorrect because if write stage is not configured, Blue Prism would not be able to identify the element.

▶ Option B is Correct by passing the windows text value, Blue Prism would be able to identify the element and write the username.

▶ Option C is incorrect because it's not required to create two elements with almost identical finger print.

▶ Option D is incorrect because write stage does not automatically identify the elements based on the value passed.

Question: 27

ANSWER: **B**

▶ Option A is not correct because read stage is used to read data from an application. The Read stage takes data from an element and stores it in a Data Item.

▶ Option B is correct because navigate stage is used to launch application.

▶ Option C is incorrect because Blue Prism does not provide stage "Attach". Attach is function provided in navigate stage.

▶ Option D is incorrect because write stage takes data (from the result of an expression) and puts it into an Application Modeller element.

Question: 28

ANSWER: **A**

▷ Option A is correct because When Match Index is set, Blue Prism will stop searching once an element has been found, instead of continuing to search for potential duplicates.

▷ Option B is incorrect because Match Reverse will make Blue Prism search in a bottom-up order rather than the default top-down order.

▷ Option C is incorrect because name attribute of element can be used to identify element uniquely. But some applications have name value same for all the elements.

▷ Option D is incorrect because value attribute should be removed from the finger print to avoid no match found error.

Question: 29

ANSWER: **D**

▷ Options A, B and C are incorrect because match type has these comparison operators.

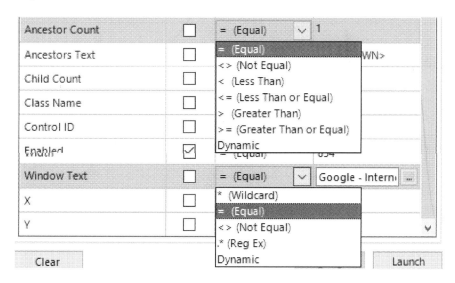

▷ Option D is correct because substring is not available as operator in match type of application modeller.

Question: 30

ANSWER: **A**

▶ Option A is correct because the statement is incorrect about work queue. Multiple robots can work on single queue.

▶ Option B, C and D all are correct about the work queue management.

Question: 31

ANSWER: **A**

▶ Option A is correct because Java access bridge should be installed for Blue Prism to spy the java applications. JAB provides the required components to Blue Prism for identifying the java elements.

▶ Option B is incorrect because SQL database is not necessary to spy the java applications.

▶ Option C is incorrect because windows access is not required to spy the applications.

▶ Option D is incorrect because Java access bridge is used to spy the java applications.

Question: 32

ANSWER: **C**

▶ Option A is incorrect because Blue Prism does not identify the data items which are placés in curly braces as data items.

▶ Option B is incorrect because Blue Prism interpret the double quotes as the string.

▶ Option C is correct because the name that is entered identifies the data item that will be displayed on the process diagram. Names of data items may not contain a full stop character ("."), quotation marks ("), or any square brackets ("[" or "]").

▶ Option D is incorrect because does not identify the data items which are places in parenthesis as data items.

Question: 33

ANSWER: **C**

▶ Option A is incorrect because Attach function is used to attach to the running application.

▶ Option B is incorrect because send key function is used to send the keys to the target application.

▶ Option C is correct because activate application function is used to activate the running application. The element should be spied using win 32 mode only.

▶ Option D is incorrect because application should be activated to send the global mouse click event to the application.

Question: 34

ANSWER: **B**

▶ Option B is correct because Blue Prism provides 5 application manager modes that are used to connect to various applications with different processor architectures.

Application Manager modes are:

1. Embedded (default)
2. External, 32-bit mode
3. External, 64-bit mode
4. External, OS address size
5. External Blue Prism address size

Question: 35

ANSWER: **D**

▶ Option A, B and C are incorrect because initial value of the date item is not configured. when this page is executed, the following error will be thrown.

▶ Option D is correct because date item initial values are not configured hence exception will be thrown while performing the calculation.

Question: 36

ANSWER: **B**

▶ Option A is incorrect because process can retry the case configurable number of times depending on the sensitivity of the applications. It does not necessarily to be 3 always.

▶ Option B is correct because exception flow is connected to main flow without clearing the exception using resume stage. This would make the process execute in recovery mode.

▶ Option C is incorrect because recovery logic does not need to be in exception block. recovery logic is in exception block and some exception happens in recovery flow, process would go into infinite exception loop.

▶ Option D is incorrect because resume stage is missing in the flow.

Question: 37

ANSWER: **A**

▶ Option A is correct cause the if a case is worked successfully, this symbol ✔ (completed)is shown next to the case.

▶ Option B is incorrect because if a case encounters an exception in its execution, the case is marked with ⚑ (Exception).

▶ Option C is incorrect because if a case is being worked, this symbol 🔒 (locked)is shown next to the case.

▶ Option D is incorrect because if a case is in pending state, the symbol ⋯ (pending) is shown next to the case.

Question: 38

ANSWER: **D**

▶ Scenario 1 - The exception stage throws a system exception if it's not placed in recovery flow.

▶ Scenario 2 - If this exception stage is placed in recovery mode, it re-throws the system exception that was raised by process.

▶ Scenario 3 -This exception stage is excluded from logging as stage logging is disable.

▶ Option D is correct since the exception stage satisfies all the three scenarios.

Question: 39

ANSWER: **C**

▶ Option A is incorrect cause the if a case is worked successfully, this symbol ✔ (completed)is shown next to the case.

▶ Option B is correct because if a case encounters an exception in its execution, the case is marked with ⚑ (Exception).

▶ Option C is incorrect because if a case is being worked, this symbol 🔒 (locked)is shown next to the case.

▶ Option D is incorrect because if a case is in pending status, symbol ⋯ (pending)is shown next to the case.

Question: 40

ANSWER: **A**

▶ Option A is correct because window text be unchecked. Note that a window could be anything from an application window to a button to a combo box item. Thus, it is necessary to think in context when considering this attribute. The WindowText of an edit field is the text that has been entered into that field.

▶ Option B is incorrect because Indicates whether the element is visible. An element may be present but invisible, care should be taken care to use this element.

▶ Option C is incorrect because Screen visible property is used to check if application screen is visible or hidden.

▶ Option D is incorrect because Class name is the name given to a type of control. This value is not changed unless the code of the application is changed.

Question: 41

ANSWER: **A**

Refer the description of the run modes:

Run Mode	
○ Foreground	If this object should never have more than one instance running at the same time on the same resource, set to Foreground. This business object can run at the same time as other background business objects.
○ Background	If this object is designed to support multiple instances running at the same time on the same resource, set to Background. This business object can run at the same time as a foreground business object or other background business objects.
● Exclusive	If this object should never be run at the same time as any other object, and requires exclusive access to the desktop, set to Exclusive. This business object can not run at the same time as any other business object.

▶ Option A is correct because background run mode objects can be run at the same time as foreground or background objects on same machine.

▶ Option B is incorrect because foreground run mode is not high priority run mode.

▶ Option C is incorrect cause setting run mode to exclusive ensure only one process runs on the resource at a time, not always.

▶ Option D is incorrect because run mode of the object is selected by default by blue prism. it can't be left blank.

Question: 42

ANSWER: A

▶ Option A is correct cause Execution will follow yes path of decision 2.

▶ Option B is incorrect cause decision1 returns false. InStr([Input],"Prism") returns 6.

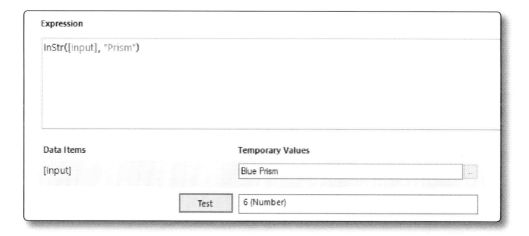

▶ Option C is incorrect because calculation stage "Set Blue Prism" is in false path of the decision2.

▶ Option D is incorrect because the process has no syntax error to throw internal exception.

Question: 43

ANSWER: C

▶ Option A is incorrect because & operator can´t be applied to numbers. Calculation stage throws invalid operation exception.

▶ Option B is incorrect because * operator performs the multiplication and process goes into infinite loop.

▶ Option C is correct because + operator adds 2 to time spent waiting data items for every run.

▶ Option D is incorrect cause of incorrect syntax in using data item.

Question: 44

ANSWER: C

▶ Option A is incorrect because internal error will be thrown mostly cause of syntax errors.

▶ Option B is incorrect because Blue Prism never stops the execution based on number of errors in process studio rather throws run time errors.

▶ Option C is correct because remove all action is called from within a loop, then the loop will not begin a new iteration after reaching the loop end stage but will continue to the next stage instead.

▶ Option D is incorrect because system exception will not be thrown.

Question: 45

ANSWERS: D

▶ Option A is correct because Process studio is right place to configure business logic and rules. Configuring logic in Process Studio gives the more control for the change management.

▶ Option B is incorrect because Object studio is used to create actions to interact with the target application using the elements which are spied by application modeller.

▶ Option C is incorrect because control room is used to perform daily executions, schedules, view queues but not to create queues.

▶ Option D is correct because system manager component is used to create work queues and its encryption key.

Question: 46

ANSWER: **B**

▶ Option A is incorrect because queue Work Queues provide a mechanism for modelling the queueing, locking and reporting of work items within a Blue Prism environment.

▶ Option B is correct because Active Queues provide a mechanism for the distribution of work amongst groups of resources and the collation of statistics and feedback to enable dynamic responses to changing workloads and business needs.

▶ Option C is incorrect because a schedule represents the point of execution of a set of tasks. Each schedule is self-contained and contains various data :- name & description, timing data and a set of tasks to perform.

▶ Option D is incorrect because session management is used to monitor the running, terminated, completed sessions in control room.

Question: 47

ANSWER: **D**

▶ Options A, B and C are not correct because work queues, collections and credentials are internal objects of Blue Prism. Internal objects cannot be debugged.

▶ Option D is correct because webservice-rest is a utility object provided by blue Prism.

Question: 48

ANSWER: **A**

- ▶ Option A is correct because Blue Prism created a utility to perform the collection related actions.

- ▶ Option B is incorrect utility-general is only used to check if process or window exists and to make the robot sleep.

- ▶ Option C is incorrect because internal collection object does not provide advanced actions such as split, transpose, filter, etc.

- ▶ Option D is incorrect because environment object is used to perform the action suck as clear clipboard, get screen resolution, get user name etc.

Question: 49

ANSWER: **D**

Tags are individual text labels which can be assigned to items. They provide a means of grouping items together and can be used to filter items in the business object or in the contents list. Get next item of the work queue used the tag file to filter the work queue cases. This can consist of any number of tag searches - each term can be separated by a semi-colon and they are all applied to the search (ie. they are AND'ed terms not OR'ed terms).

- ▶ Option D is correct because there is no limit on the number of tags we add to a case.

Question: 50

ANSWER: **C**

- ▶ Option A is incorrect because RPA can be used to read the input from complex applications.

- ▶ Option B is incorrect because RPA is not only data entry technology.

- ▶ Option C is correct because RPA is technology where software mimics the user action in very intelligent manner.

▶ Option D is incorrect because RPA is not part of artificial intelligence, RPA augments the artificial intelligence by providing the huge volumes of data.

Question: 51

ANSWER: **A**

▶ Option A is correct because public switch is used in conjunction with the /resourcepc switch only makes the resource PC publicly available.

automate /resourcepc /public

▶ Option B is incorrect because /resource switch launches the blue prism in resourcepc mode but not in public mode.

▶ Option C is incorrect because it specifies the name of the database connection to use, instead of the current one, for this session only. (i.e. the current connection is left unchanged).

▶ Option D is incorrect because automate is the name of the Blue Prism command line utility.

Question: 52

ANSWER: **C**

▶ Option A is incorrect because all the data items created on page are local by default. Visibility should be changed to global to make it visible on other pages.

▶ Option B is incorrect because statistic variables are used to save the value of data item in data base. Data items are not static by default. Exposure should be changed manually.

▶ Option C is correct because data Items are normally local and only visible to their own page.

▶ Option D is incorrect because session variables are used to control execution path. Data items should be exposed as session variables with greater consideration.

Question:53

ANSWER: **D**

▶ Option A is incorrect because Visibility of data item is local. Hence, it's not a global data item.

▶ Option B Is incorrect because exposure property of the data item is not configured as session.

▶ Option C is incorrect because number is a data item of type number. It can save any number.

▶ Option D is correct case that by default the current value is reset to the initial value when the start stage of the page is reached. When the checkbox is un-checked, the current value is maintained and not reset.

Question: 54

ANSWER: **D**

▶ Option A, B and C are not correct because Blue Prism has the below data items available:
  ● Number: used for any numerical value
  ● Text: used for any alphanumeric value
  ● Flag: used for True or False values
  ● Date: used for date values
  ● Password: used for sensitive data
  ● Datetime: used for date and time data
  ● Time: used for time values
  ● Timespan: used to store a length of time
  ● Image: used to hold an image in a Data Item
  ● Binary: used to store binary data, like the contents of a binary file

▶ Option D is correct because byte is a data item provided by the .NET, not available in Blue Prism.

Question: 55

ANSWER: **A**

▶ Option A is correct because "Page details" page is the orphaned Page Reference stage that means page is referring to deleted page.

▶ Option B is incorrect because page stage can't refer the pages from other business object. Action stage should be employed for calling pages from other objects.

▶ Option C is incorrect because page stage can't call the actions.

▶ Option D is incorrect because page is referring to deleted page.

Question: 56

ANSWER: **C**

▶ Option A is incorrect because if a business object is trying to perform action on not launched or not connected applications, below exception will be thrown.

▶ Option B is incorrect because attaching to already attached application would result in "Already attached" exception.

▶ Option C correct because business object is trying to launch the application which is already launched.

▶ Option D is incorrect because activating a window of application which is minimized would not cause the above exception.

Question: 57

ANSWER: **A**

▶ Option A is correct because an anchor stage is a visual stage and allows links to be placed at right angles around the process, preventing the process from becoming difficult to lay out on the page. It has zero effect on the execution of the process.

▶ Option B is incorrect because action stage is used to call pages in business objects. If action stage has error, it would prevent the process from successful execution.

▶ Option C is incorrect because page is used to call the pages from the same process or Business object. If page stage has error, it would prevent the process from successful execution.

▶ Option D is incorrect because a link chains together the various stages within the flowchart. If any stage is missing inbound or outbound link throws exception.

Question: 58

ANSWER: **A**

▶ Option A is correct because exception stage is used to raise the contemplated system exceptions and Business exceptions.

▶ Option B is incorrect because resume stage is used to neutralize the exception raised on the page.

▶ Option C is incorrect because recover stage is used to catch the exception raised in exception block. if exception blocks are not used, recover stage catches the exception on the page.

▶ Option D is incorrect that exception stage is used to raise the contemplated system exceptions and Business exceptions.

Question: 59

ANSWER: **A**

▶ Option A is correct because a business object includes two compulsory actions called initialise and clean up. They cannot be deleted or renamed, and no other action can share their name(s).

▶ Option B is incorrect because login and logout pages are associated with target application and should be created by user.

▶ Option C is incorrect because Launch and terminate actions are associated with target application and should be created by user.

▶ Option D is incorrect because business object includes two compulsory actions called initialise and clean up.

Question: 60

ANSWER: **C**

▶ Option A is not correct because Get Pending Items action returns all the pending cases from the work queue but does not lock any of the pending items.

▶ Option B is incorrect because Get Item Data returns the saved work case data and details of the work case but does not lock for the processing.

▶ Option C is correct because Get Next Item action returns a pending case and lock it for processing it.

▶ Option D is incorrect because Get Locked Item action returns the list of the Item IDs of the locked items.

Question: 61

ANSWER: **D**

New items can be deferred to prevent them from being worked too soon. If a deferral date is specified when items are created, the queue will hold on to them until that date. Effectively the items are temporarily frozen.

If Get Next Item fails to get an item, it does not necessarily mean there are no unworked items in the queue; it could be that there are deferred items the queue is yet to release.

Hence all the options that are mentioned are correct.

Question: 62

ANSWER: **A**

▶ Option A is correct because to calculate last day of the month, first of the month should be calculated and by adding one month to first date of current month, first day of the next month is calculated. By subtracting one day from first of the next month gives the last day of the current month.

▶ Option B is incorrect because the formula gives the first day of the current month.

▶ Option C is incorrect causer that the formula gives the last day of the last month.

▶ Option D is incorrect since option A gives the last date of the current month.

Question: 63

ANSWER: **A**

▶ Option A is correct because step through the page would execute the page in debug mode, hence developer can see the execution control executing all the steps in "open Application "Page.

▶ Option B is incorrect because step over would execute the page, but debug control would not display the execution of steps in page "Open Application".

▶ Option C is incorrect because Highlight "Read Details" stage and select "Set Next Stage" makes the process skip the execution of "Open Application" page.

▶ Option D is incorrect because it's possible to skip the execution of the stages in process.

Question: 64

ANSWER: **A**

▶ Option A is correct case that Blue Prism auto refreshes the environmental variables in all the processes with our user involvement. Hence the changes would reflect in processes immediately.

▶ Option B is incorrect because user does not need to restart the Blue Prism to apply the new value of environmental change.

▶ Option C is incorrect that user does not need to restart the machine to change the environmental variables.

▶ Option D is incorrect because the reason to use environment variables is so that minor changes to the configuration of a solution can be made without the need make development changes to the objects or processes.

Question: 65

ANSWER: **B**

▶ Option A is incorrect because process should never be terminated with unhandled exception. Terminating process without handling exception at low level is sign of bad design.

▶ Option B is correct cause the way in which an exception moves upward through the layers of a solution is known as bubbling. An exception will bubble upwards until it is handled, and if it is not handled it will eventually bubble up to the main page of the process and cause it to fail.

▶ Option C is incorrect because usage of blocks isolates the exception from bubbling to the upper layer. Exception block is used to take the exception path in case of exceptions in process.

▶ Option D is incorrect because nullifying the exception with resume stage would make the process to continue its execution.

Question: 66

ANSWER: B

▶ Option A is incorrect because process throws a system exception if the timeout expires. You may need a long timeout here to absorb any system latency.

▶ Option B is correct cause of that we would probably throw a Business Exception and determine the exception reason from the application error message e.g. invalid product code, product out of stock, etc.

▶ Option C is incorrect because validation error does not represent the intent of the message provided by the Blue Prism. Blue Prism does only recommend using system and business exceptions.

▶ Option D is incorrect because Option B is correct.

Question: 67

ANSWER: C

▶ Option A is incorrect because Blue Prism uses to identify the string (sequence of letters) parameters. Option A gives us the below result.

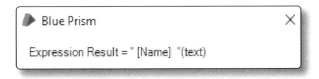

▶ Option B Is incorrect because + operator cannot be applied on string data items in Blue Prism. Below result would be returned.

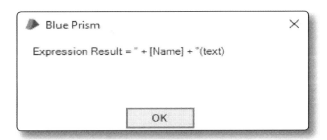

▶ Option C is correct because one should use Chr() function to derive special key board characters.

▶ Option D is incorrect because * operator cannot be applied on string values.

Question: 68

ANSWER: **B**

▶ Option A is incorrect because choice stage follows the execution path of correct choice. In below image if [value] is 1, choice stage takes the first path. If [value] is 3, choice stage takes second path.

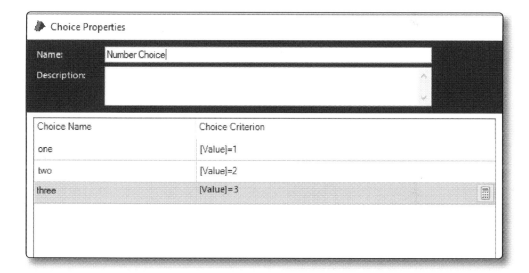

▶ Option B is correct because choice stage takes otherwise path if none of the options are correct. In above configuration, if value is not equal to 1, 2 or 3, choice stage takes otherwise path.

▶ Option C is incorrect because choice stage can't be configured with otherwise choice´.

▶ Option D is incorrect because otherwise stage gets executed when all the choices are incorrect.

Question: 69

ANSWER: D

▸ Option A is not correct because wait stage can be configured to have multiple conditions.

▸ Option B is incorrect because wait stage without condition can be used as pause in the object studio.

▸ Object C is incorrect because an exception at the timeout stage will alert the process about the exception. Process can have exception logic in process studio.

▸ Option D is correct because Time out of the wait stage can be decimal values like 0.1, 0.2, 0.3, etc.

Question: 70

ANSWER: A

▸ Option A is correct cause the by changing the stage logging to errors or disable would prevent the data of read stage being logged.

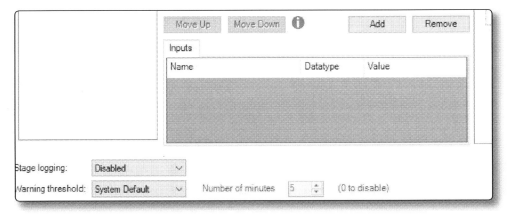

▸ Option B is incorrect that if logging is disabled on machine, all the actions of the process would not be logged making the error correction very difficult.

▸ Option C is incorrect because if bank account number saved as password, casting needs to be done in various stages where bank account is used.

▸ Option D is incorrect because Blue Prism would not detect the sensitive data.

Question: 71

ANSWER: **B**

- ▶ Option A is incorrect because process studio is a part where processes and objects can be created. In process studio process and object modification logs can be viewed. Using Process Studio - a drag and drop interface allows process flows to be quickly and easily implemented using the resources deployed on the current machine.

- ▶ Option B is correct because control room of blue prism is used to run the process on a virtual robot.

- ▶ Option C is incorrect because Object Studio is used to capture the functionality of an application so that it can be employed by Processes.

- ▶ Option D is incorrect because Object Studio has a feature called Application Modeller that enables us to create a logical representation of an application. Application Modeller is used to spy the elements of the target application.

Question: 72

ANSWER: **A**

- ▶ Option A is correct because Step button would step into the "open Application" and will pause on start stage of the page.

- ▶ Option B is incorrect because step over would execute the page, but debug control would not display the execution of steps in page "Open Application".

- ▶ Option C is incorrect because Highlight "Read Details" stage and select "Set Next Stage" makes the process skip the execution of "Open Application" page.

- ▶ Option D is incorrect because step out Continues running until the flow moves out of the current page/sub-process back to the stage which called the current page/sub-process.

Question: 73

ANSWER: **D**

▶ Option A is incorrect because start stage is used to configure input parameters.

▶ Option B is incorrect because end stage is used to configure only output parameters.

▶ Option C is incorrect because start and end stages are used to send input and output parameters to another page or another process.

▶ Option D is correct because start and end stages are used to send input and output parameters to another page or another process. In Process Studio, these inputs are shown in the properties of the Action stage.

Question: 74

ANSWER: **B**

▶ Option A is incorrect because the 'unable to match with query terms' message is Application Modeller's way of telling you it cannot find the element. Essentially it is saying 'I can't see the element that you referenced anymore'. Sample error is shown below.

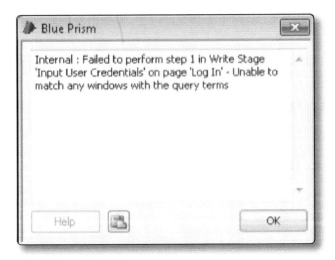

- Option B is correct because "Activate window" stage could find multiple elements conflicting with the element referenced in "Input User Credentials" stage.

- Option C is incorrect because "Input User Credentials" is read stage.

- Option D is incorrect because "Input User Credentials" is a stage used to input credentials in an application.

Question: 75

ANSWER: **B**

- Option A is incorrect because Alert stage can be configured in exception block.

- Option B correct because blocks should not overlap, and blocks cannot be nested in blue prism process design.

- Option C is incorrect because Exception stage can be configured in exception block.

- Option D is incorrect because recovery stage can be configured in exception block, but greater degree of care should be given avoid infinite loop in exception block.

Question: 76

ANSWER: **B**

- Option A is incorrect because reset button does not necessarily to be pressed after running the process.

- Option B is correct because reset the Reset button must always be pressed before re-running a process. Reset button resets all the data items in the process making the process ready for next re-run.

- Option C is incorrect because reset button can't be pressed after re-running the process.

- Option D is incorrect because without using reset button below error appear while trying to re-run the process.

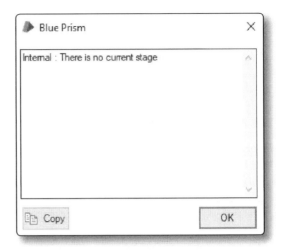

Question: 77

ANSWER: B

▶ Option A is incorrect because a write stage takes data (from the result of an expression) and puts it into an application modeller element. But its incorrect that only write stage should be used for writing passwords.

▶ Option B is correct because application should be in focus and cursor should be in password field for navigate stage to send values to password field. Navigate stage can't verify the position of the cursor, sends keys to application.

▶ Option C is incorrect because date items can be used as input to the navigate stage.

▶ Option D is incorrect because process will fail at navigate stage if application is minimized.

Question: 78

ANSWER: C

▶ Option A is incorrect because when match index is set, Blue Prism will stop searching once an element has been found, instead of continuing to search for potential duplicates. And that Match Reverse will make Blue Prism search in a bottom-up order rather than the default top-down order. Hence finding the last element.

▶ Option B is incorrect because this configuration gets the last element.

▶ Option C is incorrect because this configuration gets the first element.

▶ Option D is incorrect because option C is correct to find the first element.

Question: 79

ANSWER: **B**

▶ Option A is incorrect because Blue Prism does not provide internal,64-bit mode as application mode.

▶ Option B is correct because application manager runs in a separate process when interfacing with the target application. The application manager process is always 64 bits with mode External, 64-bit mode.

▶ Option C is incorrect because the application manager process matches the operation system address size. e.g. on 64-bit Windows, it will be a 64-bit process irrespective of the target application type.

▶ Option D is incorrect because the application manager process matches Blue Prism's address size. e.g. if Blue Prism is running as a 64-bit process, the application manager process will also be 64-bit irrespective of the target application type.

Question: 80

ANSWER: **D**

Step over and step out both can be used to execute pages in one go.

▶ Step Over: except that if the current stage is a page reference stage or a sub process then all stages contained inside the referenced page/process are executed in one go.

▶ Step Out: continues running until the flow moves out of the current page/ sub-process back to the stage which called the current page/sub-process.

Hence the answer is D.

Question: 81

ANSWER: **B**

▶ Option A is incorrect because internal error does not mean product failure. Internal exception is thrown when Blue Prism is not able to perform the action with user provided inputs.

▶ Option B is correct because if read stage is not connected other stage, the above exception is thrown.

▶ Option C is incorrect because not connected error is thrown if business object is not connected to the application.

▶ Option D is incorrect because execution does not happen to the stages which are not present in the flow.

Question: 82

ANSWER: **B**

▶ Option A is incorrect cause the if a case is worked successfully, this symbol ✓ (completed)is shown next to the case.

▶ Option B is correct because if a case encounters an exception in its execution, the case is marked with ▶ (Exception).

▶ Option C is incorrect because if a case is being worked, this symbol 🔒 (locked)is shown next to the case.

▶ Option D is incorrect because if a case is in pending status, symbol ••• (pending)is shown next to the case.

Question: 83

ANSWER: **C**

▶ Option A is incorrect because all the resources that are connected to server as public resources will respond to requests from control room.

▶ Option B is incorrect because two processes which use exclusive objects can't be executed on same machine. Error message is below.

▶ Option C is incorrect because below error is displayed if machine is offline and shutdown and the error "**Not connected**" appears if user want to run the virtual robot on the machine.

▶ Option D is incorrect because scenarios 4 is incorrect.

Question: 84

ANSWER: A

▶ Option A is incorrect because process would take the retry path as long as "time spent waiting" is less the "max time(seconds)".

▶ Option B is incorrect because process would raise the exception as "max time(seconds)" is greater than the "time spent waiting".

▶ Option C is correct because process would raise the exception as "max time(seconds)" is greater than the "time spent waiting".

▶ Option D is incorrect cause the process would take false path of decision stage as "max time(seconds)" is not equal to "TimeSpentwaiting".

Question: 85

ANSWER: **A**

▶ Option A is correct because exception in calculation stage is recovered by recover2 stage as calc1 stage is in exception block2.

▶ Option B is incorrect because the exception in calc1 stage is controlled using exception block2, hence execution will follow the recover2 flow.

▶ Option C is incorrect because execution will follow the recove2 path. If calc1 stage is not in exception block, exception would be thrown resulting termination of the process.

▶ Option D is incorrect because execution would take the recover2 path.

Question: 86

ANSWER: **C**

▶ Option A is incorrect because if action does not exist.

▶ Option B is incorrect because if application has not launched, Blue Prism throws not launched exception.

▶ Option C is correct because action waited for configurable time to identify the element and threw the exception back to process after wait time.

▶ Option D is incorrect because login action is not performed application navigation.

Question: 87

ANSWER: **C**

▶ Option A is incorrect because of the incorrect syntax of using data item in calculation.

▶ Option B is incorrect cause of incorrect syntax of using collection in calculation.

▶ Option c is correct because if getnextitem does not find pending items in queue, it returns itemID (text) as null.

▶ Option D is incorrect because operators can't be applied directly on collections like data items.

Question: 88

ANSWER: **B**

> ▶ Option A is incorrect because get next item is used to get the pending items from the queue.

> ▶ Option B is correct because" add to queue" action is used to add the cases to queue.

> ▶ Option C is incorrect because set data is used to add data to existing queue case item.

> ▶ Option D is incorrect because defer action is used to defer the case to be worked in future.

Question: 89

ANSWER: **C**

> ▶ Option A is incorrect because queue Work Queues provide a mechanism for modelling the queueing, locking and reporting of work items within a Blue Prism environment.

> ▶ Option B is incorrect because Active Queues provide a mechanism for the distribution of work amongst groups of resources and the collation of statistics and feedback to enable dynamic responses to changing workloads and business needs.

> ▶ Option C is correct because a schedule represents the point of execution of a set of tasks. Each schedule is self-contained and contains various data :- name & description, timing data and a set of tasks to perform.

> ▶ Option D is incorrect because session management is used to monitor the running, terminated, completed sessions in control room.

Question: 90

ANSWER: **A**

> ▶ Option A is correct cause the un checking "Hide from other pages in the process" makes the data item a global variable that is visible in all the pages.

▶ Option B is incorrect because selection of static in exposure drop down makes the data item a static data item.

▶ Option C is incorrect because selection of session in exposure drop down makes the data item a session data item.

▶ Option D is incorrect because unchecking "reset to initial value when this page runs" make the data items have the value from last execution.

Question: 91

ANSWER: **A**

▶ Option A is correct because dot notation is used to refer to collection fields, i.e. 'Collection Name.Field Name'.

▶ Option B is incorrect cause of wrong syntax.

▶ Option C is incorrect cause of wrong syntax.

▶ Option D is incorrect because if characters are passed in "", Blue Prism would treat them as text.

Question: 92

ANSWER: **B**

▶ Option A is incorrect because if Business object is trying to perform action on not launched or not connected applications, below exception will be thrown.

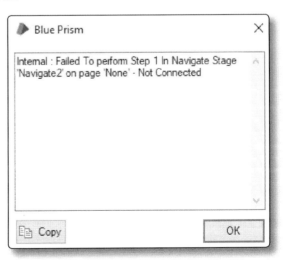

▶ Option B is correct because attaching to already attached application would result in "already attached" exception i.e. mentioned in question.

▶ Option C correct because business object is trying to launch the application which is already launched.

▶ Option D is incorrect because activating a window of application which is minimized would not cause the above exception.

Question: 93

ANSWER: **A**

▶ Option A is correct because breakpoints only take effect when the diagram is open. In the Production environment, the diagram is not displayed when a process runs, and breakpoints are ignored.

▶ Option B is incorrect because in execution environment breakpoints are ignored and execution continues as usual.

▶ Option C is incorrect because break points in code does not prevent the robot from being executed from control room on virtual robot.

▶ Option D is incorrect because break points in code does not prevent the robot from being visible in control room.

Question: 94

ANSWER: **C**

▶ Option A is incorrect because mark as completed is not a default page in Blue Prism process. A separate process can be created to mark the cases as completed and to change the status of the tag.

▶ Option B is incorrect because mark as exception is not a default page in Blue Prism process. A separate process can be created to mark the cases as exception and to set the exception reason.

▶ Option C is correct because Main is the page that is created by default and can't be renamed and deleted. Below are the properties of the main page.

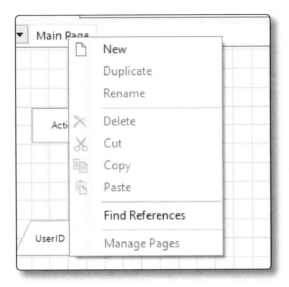

▶ Option D is incorrect because load queue is page defined in Blue Prism template. But it's not a mandatory page. Queue loading logic can be implemented in another page as per the process business logic.

Question: 95

ANSWER: **D**

▶ Scenario 1 is correct case that stepping into an action stage will open object studio and stepping out will close it.

▶ Scenario 2 is correct because stepping into a process reference stage will open another process studio window in a similar way to the setting into the action stage.

▶ Scenario 3 is correct because business object flows through pages one at a time.

▶ Scenario 4 is correct because process uses action stage to call employee a Business object page.

▶ Hence correct option is D.

Question: 96

ANSWER: **D**

 ▶ Option A is incorrect because alert stage is used to send the alerts to the users in case of unexpected events.

 ▶ Option B is incorrect because exception stage is used to throw the exceptions. It does not need to be followed by resume stage.

 ▶ Option C is incorrect exception block is independent stage.

 ▶ Option D is correct because recovery stage should be followed by resume stage. resume stage is used to clear the exception when flows is connected to normal execution flow.

Question: 97

ANSWER: **B**

 ▶ Option A is incorrect because attach action throws exception if object tries to attach again to already attached application.

 ▶ Option B is correct because attach action throws exception if object tries to attach again to already attached application. To avoid the exception, always its recommended to check already connected flag. The attach action should be as below:

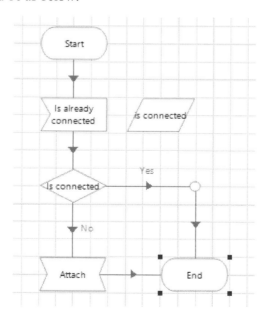

▶ Option C is incorrect because attach action does not launch the application.

▶ Option D is incorrect because navigate stage is used to launch and attach to already launched application.

Question: 98

ANSWER: **C**

▶ Option A is incorrect because if process is trying to launch the application which is already launched, "Already launched application" exception would be thrown.

▶ Option B is incorrect because if a process is trying to attach to the application which is already attached, "already attached" exception will be thrown. Below is the exception image.

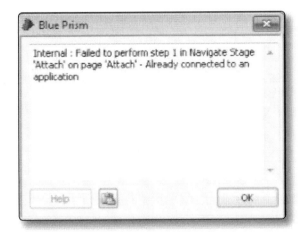

▶ Option C is correct because the mentioned exception raised when process is trying to attach to the application which is not launched.

▶ Option D is incorrect because if the process was not able to identify the window, "no element found" exception will be thrown.

Question: 99

ANSWER: **B**

▶ Scenario 1 is incorrect because pages in business object can be published to process studio to be called using actin stage.

▶ Scenario 2 is correct because page has not been published to be called from process studio.

▶ Scenario 3 is incorrect because pages can be called in another page of business object and can be published to process studio as well.

▶ Scenario 4 is incorrect because Blue Prism does not provide any functionality to hide the pages in Blue Prism.

Question: 100

ANSWER: **C**

▶ Option A and B are incorrect because functions like ExceptionDetail() and ExceptionType() can be used in any page either in process or in Business object.

▶ Option C is correct because Exception functions like ExceptionDetail() and ExceptionType() cannot be used anywhere other than in between a Recover and a Resume, i.e. in Recovery Mode.

▶ Option D is incorrect because ExceptionDetails () function can't be used outside of recovery mode.

Question: 101

ANSWER: **A**

▶ Option A is correct because the keep locked input parameter works in conjunction with the retry input. When Keep Locked is true the new cloned item will become instantly locked.

▶ Option B is incorrect because the new closed item will be locked as the input parameter of mark as exception action "Keep Locked" is true.

▶ Option C is incorrect because current case is not marked as completed.

▶ Option D is incorrect because current case is not marked as completed.

Question: 102

ANSWER: **B**

▶ Option A is incorrect because all the resources that are connected to server as public resources will respond to requests from control room.

▶ Option B is correct because two processes which use exclusive objects can't be executed on same machine.

▶ Option C is incorrect because below error is displayed if machine is offline and shutdown.

Name	State	Session Info	Members	Connecti
	Offline			No

▶ Option D is incorrect because scenarios 2 and 3 are incorrect.

Question: 103

ANSWER: **A**

▶ Option A is correct because a process or business object can be exported as an XML file, and similarly an exported file can be imported into Blue Prism.

▶ Option B is incorrect because Blue Prism does not use XSLT file type for exporting. UIPath uses this file type for saving processes.

▶ Option C is incorrect because bprelease file types are created Blue Prism for making releases which can be imported in another environment.

▶ Option D is incorrect because cs file types belongs to .NET.

Question: 104

ANSWER: **D**

▶ Option D is correct because all the options A, B and C are true.

▶ Option A statement is right because environmental variables can be accessed from processes or objects.

▶ Option B statement is right because environmental variables are read-only variables can't be overridden.

▶ Option C statement is right because name of the data items should match with the name of the environmental variable else Blue Prism cannot load the environment variable into data item.

Question: 105

ANSWER: C

▶ Option A is incorrect because session variables are specific to the sessions. Changes in one session would not impact the other session.

▶ Option B is incorrect because reading session variable before another robot does not define the value.

▶ Option C is correct because session variables are specific to that instance of the Process. If 2 instances of the same process are running at the same time, they will both have the same Session Variables, but the Session Variables will have different values.

▶ Option D is incorrect because session variables are specific to the sessions.

Question: 106

ANSWER: B

▶ Option A is incorrect because control room is used to monitor the ongoing process executions and session logs, schedulers ,etc. From control room, one can't unlock the orphaned environmental locks.

▶ Option B is correct because When an unexpected crash or power cut interrupts a Process, one will not be able to rely on the software to automatically release the lock. In such cases one will need to manually intervene in System Manager to release the lock.

▶ Option C is incorrect because process studio is used to create the processes.

▶ Option D is incorrect because object studio is used to create objects.

Question: 107

ANSWER: B

▶ Option A is incorrect because current case is marked as exception and new case is not created as "retry" parameter of mark as exception action is false.

▶ Option B is correct because the retry input parameter of the Mark Exception action in the Internal - Work Queues Business Object can then be used to override max attempts.

▶ Option C is incorrect because current case will not be retried without making case as exception.

▶ Option D is incorrect because current case is marked as exception.

Question: 108

OPTIONS: A

▶ Option A is correct because Blue Prism uses the grid tool to identify rectangular areas of the screen. Application modeller does this by superimposing a grid onto the application to make the rows and columns of the screen visible. One unit of the grid represents one character space on the screen.

▶ Option B is incorrect because JAB (Java access bridge) is used to connect to java applications.

▶ Option C is incorrect because AA (active accessibility) is used to interact with some windows type complex applications.

▶ Option D is incorrect because Spy++ has a toolbar and hyperlinks to help you work faster. It also provides a **Refresh** command to update the active view, a **Window Finder Tool** to make spying easier.

Question: 109

ANSWER: **C**

▶ Option A is incorrect because GetSessionId() function is used to get the id of current running session. This session id can be used to control the session using commands.

▶ Option B is incorrect because singleSignon() function is used to verify if data base is configured with single sign on or not.

▶ Option C is correct because IsStopRequested() is used to verify if user requested stop from control room.

▶ Option D is incorrect because IsImmediateStopRequested() is not a function supported by blue prism.

Question: 110

ANSWER: **D**

▶ Option A, B and C are incorrect because code stage, wait stage and read stage are unique to object studio. They are not present in process studio.

▶ Option D is correct because alert stage is inly present in process studio, not present in object studio.

Question:111

ANSWER: **C**

▶ Option A is incorrect because Blue prism work queue can have duplicate cases.

▶ Option B is incorrect because get next item action of work queue object does not verify if duplicate pending cases are present in work queue.

▶ Option C is correct because the mechanism to avoid duplicates should be implemented in process logic. "Is item in queue "should be called and should be verified if case not present in queue before adding it to queue.

▶ Option D is incorrect because manual work is not required to delete duplicate cases from queue.

Question: 112

ANSWER: **C**

▶ Option A is incorrect because collections are used to perform operations on Blue Prism collections.

▶ Option B is incorrect because Blue prism has no internal object called "Scheduler". Scheduler Is a functionality of Blue Prism server and can be configured in control room.

▶ Option C is correct because calendars internal object is used to perform operations on calendars. Refer below image for all the actions of calendars object.

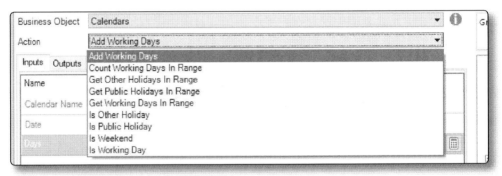

▶ Option D is incorrect because Blue Prism has no internal object called "Task". Task is a part of Blue Prism scheduler and can be configured in control room.

Question: 113

ANSWER: **B**

▶ Option A is incorrect because read stage can over write the initial values in its execution.

▶ Option B is correct because Blue Prism was not able to convert the text to number.

▶ Option C is incorrect because button text values would not impact the cast.

▶ Option D is incorrect because internal exceptions are not caused by BP failure.

Question: 114

ANSWER: **C**

▶ Option A, B and D are incorrect because Blue Prism uses 8181 for launching resourcePC if another port is not mentioned in command line.

▶ Option C is correct because BP resource pc is launched on 8181 by default. If the default port of 8181 is already used for another service on your network, you may wish to use another. Be sure to use the same port for all resource PCs on your network, unless you have a specific reason not to do this.

Question: 115

ANSWER: **A**

▶ Option A is correct because step over button would step into the "open Application" and will pause on start stage of the page since a break point is set up.

▶ Option B is incorrect because step over would execute the page, but debug control would not display the execution of steps in page "Open Application" if there are no breakpoints set up in the page/sub-process.

▶ Option C is incorrect because Highlight "Read Details" stage and select "Set Next Stage" makes the process skip the execution of "Open Application" page.

▶ Option D is correct because Step Out Continues running until the flow moves out of the current page/sub-process back to the stage which called the current page/sub-process.

Question: 116

ANSWER: **B**

▶ Option A is incorrect is because Blue Prism server is the main component in Blue Prism RPA infrastructure set up. Blue Prism server behaves as central piece for all the robots in one environment.

▶ Option B is correct because login agent service is used to make remote login.

▶ Option C is incorrect because resourcepc is another mode of Blue Prism to execute the processes. In Resource PC mode, Blue Prism functions as a Resource PC, listening for instructions from remote instances of Control Room. To run more than one Resource PC on a single machine (or to run a Resource PC at the same time as running in Interactive mode), any additional Resource PC instances must be launched specifying a different port number.

▶ Option D is incorrect cause the controllerPC is the workstation of process controller. ControllerPC is used to send commands to robots and to monitor them.

Question: 117

ANSWER: **B**

▶ Option A is incorrect because stage logging can be disabled or enabled as per the necessity.

▶ Option B is correct because Warning threshold is set to 5 min which is default.

▶ Option C is incorrect because Warning threshold is not disabled on read stage.

▶ Option D is incorrect because internal exception will not be thrown while executing this read stage.

Question: 118

ANSWER: **A**

▶ Option A is correct because Starting is not a valid session status that's shown in control room.

▶ Option B, C and D are incorrect cause the they are valid session statuses of session. refer the following status diagram.

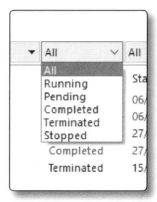

Question: 119

ANSWER: **B**

▶ Option A is incorrect because control room is used to monitor the running robots and to control the executions.

▶ Option B is correct because credentials are created in system manager of Blue Prism.

▶ Option C is incorrect because analytics tab is used to demonstrate statistics of Blue Prism environment.

▶ Option D is incorrect release manager is used to keep track of all the release that happened in environment.

Question:120

ANSWER: **C**

▶ Option A is not correct because credential object is provided to save, retrieve and set the credentials in credential manager. It encrypts passwords internally but does not expose functionality to encrypt the data items.

- Option B is incorrect because work queues object provides the actions to be performed on work queues and does not expose action to encrypt the data items.
- Option C is correct because this object is provided by blue prism in its recent versions to encrypt data items. Encryption scheme should be passed as input to all the actions of this object.
- Option D is incorrect because encryption object is used to encrypt the data items.

Question: 121

ANSWER: D

- Option A is incorrect because global timeout numbers for an application can be configured as environmental variable, so they can be amended easily.
- Option B is incorrect because the URL for a browser application would be different for different environments. Hence it should be configured as environmental variable.
- Option C is incorrect because the mails of Business users are very prone to changes, hence they should be configured to avoid the code changes.
- Option D is correct because work queue data such as name of work queue, name of primary key can't be changed frequently hence user does not need to configure in environmental variable.

Question: 122

ANSWER: B

- Option A is incorrect because step through the page would execute the page in debug mode, hence developer can see the execution control executing all the steps in "open Application "page.
- Option B is correct because step over would execute the page, but debug control would not display the execution of steps in page "Open Application".

▶ Option C is incorrect because Highlight "Read Details" stage and select "Set Next Stage" makes the process skip the execution of "Open Application" page.

▶ Option D is incorrect because it's possible to skip the execution of the stages in process.

Questions: 123

ANSWER: C

▶ Option A is incorrect because IsStopRequested is native function of Blue Prism and does not verify if code has end stage or not.

▶ Option B is incorrect because Killing Blue Prism from Task Manager abruptly shuts down robot.

▶ Option C is correct because IsStopRequest is used to check if a safe stop has been requested from control room and to stop the robot without disturbing the work queue.

▶ Option D is incorrect that Robot does not notify user to stop robot using IsStopRequested.

Question: 124

ANSWER: D

▶ Option A is incorrect because an exception generated inside a Block will be handled by the Recover inside that Block, but it does not necessary always to keep recovery stage in exception block.

▶ Option B is incorrect because resume stage nullifies the exception to make process go ahead with the normal execution. But resume stage is not necessary in case of rethrowing the exception.

▶ Option C is incorrect because more than one recover stage can be used in a process.

▶ Option D is correct because One Recover stage will handle all exceptions on a page. Hence any extra Recover stages than one on a page will be superfluous.

Question: 125

ANSWER: **D**

▶ Option D is correct because by dividing the process logic into subpages, following concepts can be achieved in code:

- Readability and reusability- It is easier to quickly understand what a process does just by looking at the Main Page. And subpages can be used to reuse the code components eliminating the use of duplicate code.

- Maintainability – Proper use of sup pages can give the developer opportunity to make modification as part of change management.

- Better exception handling – As per the blue prism best practice guide, exceptions should be handled in subpages to avoid the retrying of entire process.

Question: 126

ANSWER: **B**

▶ Option A is incorrect because Step button would step into the "open Application" and will pause on start stage of the page.

▶ Option B is correct because step over would execute the page, but debug control would not display the execution of steps in page "Open Application".

▶ Option C is incorrect because Highlight "Read Details" stage and select "Set Next Stage" makes the process skip the execution of "Open Application" page.

▶ Option D is incorrect because Step Out Continues running until the flow moves out of the current page/sub-process back to the stage which called the current page/sub-process.

Question: 127

ANSWER: **A**

▶ Option A is correct because an Action stage allows us to use a Business Object in a Process.

▶ Option B is incorrect because action stage is not used to perform actions on excel application. MS Excel VBO is used to do perform excel operations.

▶ Option C is incorrect because action stage is not used to navigate application. Page in object studio would facilitate to navigate through application using the spied elements.

▶ Option D is incorrect because navigate stage is used to launch the application.

Question: 128

ANSWER: **A**

▶ Option A is correct because when match index is set, Blue Prism will stop searching once an element has been found, instead of continuing to search for potential duplicates. And that Match Reverse will make Blue Prism search in a bottom-up order rather than the default top-down order.

▶ Option B is incorrect because match reverse will make Blue Prism search in a bottom-up order rather than the default top-down order and Blue Prism keep on searching till it finds the first element.

▶ Option C is incorrect because this configuration gets the first element.

▶ Option D is incorrect because option A is correct to find the last element.

Question: 129

ANSWER: **C**

▶ Option A is incorrect because control room is used to monitor the work queues and scheduling purposes.

▶ Option B is incorrect because processes are created in an area of Blue Prism called Process Studio.

▶ Option C is correct because the purpose of application modeller is to capture details of elements of the application user interface, things like fields, buttons and windows. Once we have defined the elements we want to use, we can set about creating a diagram to interact with them.

▶ Option D is incorrect because object studio is used to capture the functionality of an application so that it can be employed by Processes.

Question: 130

ANSWER: A

▶ Option A is correct because initial value of the date item is configured as one and calculation gets executed for number of elements in collection i.e. 4. Below is the calculation that is done by blue prism.

Result = (((1*1) *2) *3) *4 = 24

▶ Option B, C and D are incorrect because date item initial values are not configured hence exception will be thrown while performing the calculation.

Question: 131

ANSWER: B

▶ Option A is incorrect because end stage does accept the inbound link. But does not accept the outbound link.

▶ Option B is correct case that start stage does not accept inbound link, but it does accept out bound link.

▶ Option C is incorrect because navigate stage does accept inbound and outbound links.

▶ Option D is incorrect because Alert stage does accept inbound and outbound links.

Question: 132

ANSWER: D

▶ Option A is incorrect cause the if a case is worked successfully, this symbol ✔ (completed)is shown next to the case.

▶ Option B is correct because if a case encounters an exception in its execution, the case is marked with ▶ (Exception).

▶ Option C is incorrect because if a case is being worked, this symbol 🔒 (locked)is shown next to the case.

▶ Option D is incorrect because if a case is in pending status, symbol ••• (pending)is shown next to the case.

Question: 133

ANSWER: D

▶ Option A is incorrect cause Execution will follow yes path of decision 2, but the syntax of calculation stage to use text is incorrect.

▶ Option B is incorrect cause decision1 returns false. InStr([Input],"Prism") return 6.

▶ Option C is incorrect because calculation stage "Set Blue Prism" is in false path of the decision2.

▶ Option D is correct because Option A is incorrect cause Execution will follow yes path of decision 2, but the syntax of calculation stage to use text is incorrect and following error will be thrown.

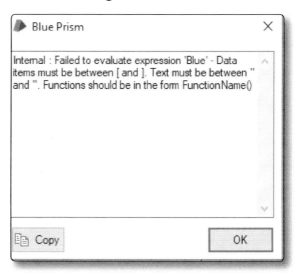

Question: 134

ANSWER: B

Refer the description of the run modes:

Run Mode

○ Foreground   If this object should never have more than one instance running at the same
time on the same resource, set to Foreground. This business object can run at
the same time as other background business objects.

○ Background   If this object is designed to support multiple instances running at the same time
on the same resource, set to Background. This business object can run at the
same time as a foreground business object or other background business
objects.

◉ Exclusive   If this object should never be run at the same time as any other object, and
requires exclusive access to the desktop, set to Exclusive. This business object
can not run at the same time as any other business object.

▶ Option B is correct because all utility objects can be run parallel with other objects of type foreground or background.

Question: 135

ANSWER: D

▶ Option A is incorrect because public switch is Used in conjunction with the /resourcepc switch only makes the resource PC publicly available.

▶ Option B is incorrect because /resource switch launches the blue prism in resourcepc mode but not in public mode.

▶ Option C is incorrect because it specifies the name of the database connection to use, instead of the current one, for this session only. (i.e. the current connection is left unchanged).

▶ Option D is correct because automateC is the name of the Blue Prism command line utility.

Question: 136

ANSWER: **A**

- ▶ Option A is correct because dot notation is used to refer to Collection fields, i.e. 'Collection Name.Field Name'. and when used in calculation field should be enclosed in [].

- ▶ Option B is incorrect cause of wrong syntax in using collection fields. Blue Prism does uses () for functions like .Net.

- ▶ Option C is incorrect cause of the wrong syntax.

- ▶ Option D is incorrect because Blue Prism interprets characters in "" as text.

Question: 137

ANSWER: **A**

- ▶ Option A is correct because encryption is an internal object of Blue Prism and Encryption object cannot be debugged.

- ▶ Options B, C and D are not correct because utility-environment, utility-general and webservices-rest are utility objects provided by blue Prism.

Question: 138

ANSWER: **B**

- ▶ Option A is incorrect cause the un checking "Hide from other pages in the process" makes the data item a global variable that is visible in all the pages.

- ▶ Option B is correct because selection of static in exposure drop down makes the data item a static data item.

- ▶ Option C is incorrect because selection of Session in exposure drop down makes the data item a session data item.

- ▶ Option D is incorrect because unchecking "reset to initial value when this page runs" make the data items have the value from last execution.

Question: 139

ANSWER: **D**

The Wait stage used to enable a business object to pause and wait for an application element. A wait stage has a timeout value which defines the maximum time it is prepared to wait for a condition. If the condition does not occur within the given time, the wait stage will direct the flow via the end. A wait stage can be stretched out to accommodate lots of different conditions, providing separate paths to take according to each condition. By using a wait stage without any condition, we can use the timeout as a positive outcome that simply delays the flow slightly.

▶ Hence option D is correct.

Question: 140

ANSWER: **D**

▶ Scenario 1 is correct because process does not contain the application logic.

▶ Scenario 2 is correct because Business object encapsulate the functionality of application using application modeller and exposes it to process studio.

▶ Scenario 3 is not correct because process studio can't not interact with target applications.

▶ Scenario 4 is correct because Business object is used to manipulate the application.

▶ Hence the correct option is D.

Question: 141

ANSWER: **A**

▶ Option A is correct because process executes the "button click" action at full speed in production environment. If targets application is slow in loading, Button click action would fails with "not found element" exception. Button click action should be implemented using wait stage as shown below.

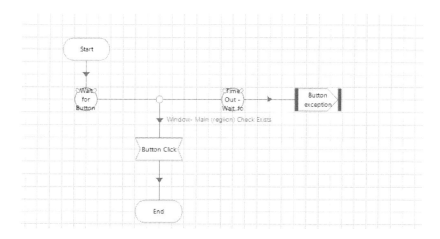

► Option B is incorrect because button click action does not wait for the search bar element loaded on application.

► Option C is incorrect because "Button Click" action does not get executed successfully even "search bar" element is not loaded. In this case button click action throws exception.

Question: 142

ANSWER: C

► Scenario 1 is correct because if a published page in business object has been deleted, process cannot identify the action.

► Scenario 2 is correct because if a published page in business object has been unpublished, process cannot identify the action.

► Scenario 3 is correct because if a published page in business object has been renamed, process cannot identify the action.

► Scenario 4 is incorrect because pages of business object can be called from multiple actions.

► Hence option C is correct.

Question: 143

ANSWER: B

> ▶ Option A is incorrect because the keep locked input parameter works in conjunction with the retry input. When keep locked is true the new cloned item will become instantly locked.

> ▶ Option B is correct because the when keep locked is false any new item created is freely available as the 'next' item.

> ▶ Option C is incorrect because current case is not marked as completed.

> ▶ Option D is incorrect because current case is not marked as completed.

Question: 144

ANSWER: D

When a business object launches an application, its attached automatically.

Attach will fail with below error if process tries to attach to the application which is already attached.

Attach actin need "Windows Title" and "Process Name" as inputs to attach.

In some scenarios, the target application may already be running, and we want to make use of that instance rather than try to start another. Similarly, some systems require that the user first logs into a 'parent' application that will then start the target application as a 'child'.

▶ Hence the correct answer is D

Question: 145

ANSWER: C

▶ Option A is incorrect because internal error does not mean product failure. Internal exception is thrown when Blue Prism is not able to perform the action with user provided inputs.

▶ Option B is incorrect because if read stage is not connected other stage, following error is thrown.

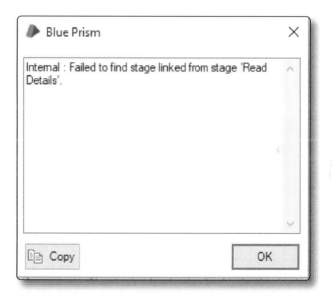

▶ Option C is correct because not connected error is thrown if Business object is not connected to the application.

▶ Option D is incorrect because execution does not happen to the stages which are not present in the flow.

Question: 146

ANSWER: D

▶ Option D is correct because options A, B and C are true.

▶ Option A is true because session variables do not need to configure in system manager. Session variables can be created in pages of process or objects.

▶ Option B is true because session variables can't be writable. Process controller can modify the value of session variables while robot is in execution.

▶ Option C is true because session variables can be viewed from and modified from control room.

Question: 147

ANSWER: D

▶ Option A, B and C are not correct because Blue Prism has native application connectors for Windows, Java-based, Browser based and mainframe applications.

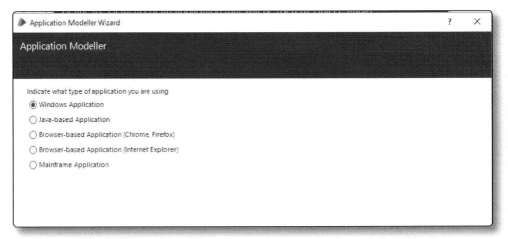

▶ Option D is correct because Blue Prism does not provide the native application connector for Data Base applications.

Question: 148

ANSWER: **A**

▶ Option A is correct because current case is marked as exception and new case is created as "retry" parameter of mark as exception action is true.

▶ Option B is incorrect because the retry input parameter of the Mark Exception action in the Internal - Work Queues business object can then be used to override max attempts. If "retry" parameter of mark as exception action is false, new clone will not be created for the current case.

▶ Option C is incorrect because current case will not be retried without making case as exception.

▶ Option D is incorrect because current case is marked as exception.

Question: 149

ANSWER: **C**

▶ Option A is incorrect because a process or business object can be exported as an XML file, and similarly an exported file can be imported into Blue Prism.

▶ Option B is incorrect because Blue Prism does not use XSLT file type for exporting. UIPath uses this file type for saving processes.

▶ Option C is correct because bprelease file types are created Blue Prism for making releases which can be imported in another environment.

▶ Option D is incorrect because CS file types belongs to .NET.

Question: 150

ANSWER: **D**

▶ Option a, B and C are incorrect because "priority" input parameter of case is not specified hence Blue Prism would consider the default priority for new cases.

▶ Option D is correct because lower numbers represent higher priorities. The default is 0 since no value is specified for "priority" input parameter of case.

Question: 151

ANSWER: C

- ▶ Option A is incorrect because if acquire lock action fails with internal exception, process would be terminated.

- ▶ Option B is incorrect because "Preferred Token" input variable Is not mandatory for "Acquire lock "action.

- ▶ Option C is correct cause if lock is acquired by other session, output of acquire lock action will be empty.

- ▶ Option D is incorrect because token is empty as session is not able to acquire lock.

Question: 152

ANSWER: A

- ▶ Option A is correct because page accepts only one start stage and multiple end stages.

- ▶ Option B is incorrect because page does not accept more than one start stage.

- ▶ Option C is incorrect because page does not accept more than one start stage.

- ▶ Option D is incorrect because all the pages by default have one start stage.

Question: 153

ANSWER: A

- ▶ Option A is correct because application time out parameter determines how long Blue Prism waits for the target application to respond before throwing an exception. This parameter only applies if the application manager mode is set to one of the external modes.

- ▶ Option B is incorrect because application time out parameter does not wait to launch the application. Navigate stage is used to launch the application.

▶ Option C is incorrect because application time out parameter does not wait to send keys to the application. Navigate stage is used to send keys to the application.

▶ Option D is incorrect because option A defines the application time out parameter usage.

Question: 154

ANSWER: **B**

▶ Option A is incorrect because exception stage is used to raise the exceptions.

▶ Option B is correct because an alert stage allows the user to raise bespoke process alerts at strategic points in a process (see Process Alerts overview for more information). When an alert stage is executed it will send a specified message to users.

▶ Option C is incorrect because action, calculation or decision stage are used to perform string calculations.

▶ Option D is incorrect because action, calculation or decision stage are used to perform collection calculations.

Question: 155

ANSWER: **B**

▶ Option A is incorrect because GetSessionId() gets the ID of the session running the current process, or empty text if no session is currently running.

▶ Option B is correct because SingleSignOn() determine if SingleSignon is being used, rather than Blue Prism authentication. True if so.

▶ Option C is incorrect because GetOSArchitecture() gets the operating system architecture.

▶ Option D is incorrect because GetConnection() gets the name of the current Blue Prism database connection.

Question: 156

ANSWER: C

▶ Option A is incorrect because SQL authentication uses credentials of an SQL user to access the database and Blue Prism scheduler can't be used using this connection type.

▶ Option B is incorrect because Availability Group uses the corresponding SQL Server options, but connect to a SQL Server Availability Group. The Server Name refers to the Availibity Group Listener.

▶ Option C is correct because connection to a dedicated Blue Prism server is the most secure connection configuration and Blue Prism scheduler can only be used using this connection type.

▶ Option D is incorrect because Windows Authentication uses the currently logged on windows user credentials to access the database. Access must be granted on the database server to allow the Windows user to access the database can't be used for scheduling purpose.

Question: 157

ANSWER: D

▶ Option A, B and C are not correct cause Blue Prism has several modes of operation, each of which can be selected using command-line options. These three are modes of Blue Prism resourcePc :

● Interactive Mode
● Resource PC Mode
● Command Mode

▶ Option D is correct because Robot Mode does not exist for Blue Prism resource PC.

Question: 158

ANSWER: C

▶ Option A is incorrect because the expression InStr("Blue Prism", "Prism") would return 6 throwing the exception in decision stage. Below exception would be thrown.

- ▶ Option B is incorrect because the expression InStr("Blue Prism", "Prism") would return 6 , not zero hence decision stage would follow false path.

- ▶ Option C is correct because the expression InStr("Blue Prism", "Prism") would return 6 , which is greater than hence decision stage would follow true path.

- ▶ Option D is incorrect because though substring function is not available, instr() function can be used to check if substring exists or not.

Question: 159

ANSWER: **C**

- ▶ Option A, B and D are incorrect because Special characters should be enclosed in curly braces (e.g. {SPACE}, {ESC}, {PGUP}, {PGDN}, {LEFT}, {RIGHT}, {UP}, {DOWN}).

- ▶ Option C is correct because special key enter is enclosed in curly braces. {ENTER} is passed as input to the send key event function.

Question: 160

ANSWER: **D**

- ▶ Option A, B and C are incorrect because windows clipboard, adobe API, saving to other format are easy picks for reading PDF documents.

- ▶ Option D is correct because OCR engine is not required to read the PDF text document.

Question: 161

ANSWER: **A**

- ▶ Statement 1 is correct because tags can be added to queue while adding it to queue.

- ▶ Statement 2 is true that tags can be removed or added using work queue internal object.

- ▶ Statement 3 is not true because can be removed or added using work queue internal object.

- ▶ Statement 4 is not true because tags will not impact the priority of the work queue case.

Question: 162

ANSWER: **B**

- ▶ Option A is incorrect because GetNextItem tag filter can be used to filter the work queue cases. If one used tag filer GetNextItem applies tag every time it gets the case from workqueue.

- ▶ Option B is correct because Using GetNextItem to get itemID and using GetItemData to get the details of case is better way to define the tag of the case to take different execution paths.

- ▶ Option C is incorrect because getItemData needs the itemId as input parameter, cannot be used independently.

- ▶ Option D is incorrect because GetItemData is used to get the tag details.

Question: 163

▶ **Answer:** B

▶ Option A is incorrect because tag is used to group the work queue cases.

▶ Option B is correct because status is used to record what work has been done so far on a Work Queue item so that work steps can't not be repeated.

▶ Option C is incorrect because priority is used to prioritize the queue cases when taking from queue to be worked.

▶ Option D is incorrect because key is configured to uniquely identify the work case.

Question: 164

ANSWER: A

Below is the role matrix of Blue Prism delivery road map.

Document	Created By
Initial Process Analysis	Blue Prism analyst or Blue Prism developer
Process Definition Document	Client SME and/or Blue Prism analyst
Functional Requirements Questionnaire	Client SME and/or Blue Prism analyst
Solution Design Document	Blue Prism developer
Operational Impact Document	Blue Prism analyst
Process Design Instruction	Blue Prism developer
Object Design Instruction	Blue Prism developer

▶ Hence the correct answer is A.

Question: 165

ANSWER: B

▶ Option A is incorrect because get cell value action gets the value of the specified cell - note that if the cell has some formatting set in it, this does *not* return the formatted value.

▶ Option B is correct because get worksheet as collection action reads all entire content of excel to Blue Prism collection.

▶ Option C is incorrect because cut action is used cut the entire workbook.

▶ Option D is incorrect because import CSV is used to import the csv as excel into Blue Prism.

Question: 166

ANSWER: **A**

▶ Option A is correct because CTRL + Right Click is used to exit the spy mode.

▶ Option B is incorrect because CTRL + Left click is used to spy the element of the application.

▶ Option C and D are incorrect because SHIT+CTRL and SHIFT +ENTER keys are not associated with any of the functionalities.

Question: 167

ANSWER: **A**

▶ Option A is correct because casting is when a value of one data type is automatically transformed to a different data type.

▶ Option B is incorrect because remove space in text is called trimming or removing empty spaces.

▶ Option C is incorrect because searching in a string is not called casting.

▶ Option D is incorrect because wrong usage of data items types can cause the casting exceptions.

Question: 168

ANSWER: **A**

▶ Option A is correct because navigate stage has native function "Global Mouse Click" to send mouse clicks to applications.

▶ Option B is incorrect because read stage is used to read the values from application.

▶ Option C is incorrect because write stage is used to write values to target application.

▶ Option D is incorrect because action stage is used to call the page of another business object.

Question: 169

ANSWER: **B**

▶ Option A is incorrect because actives ques are used to allocated resources based on queue load.

▶ Option B is correct because resource Pools are used to group the resource pcs of Blue Prism environment.

▶ Option C is incorrect because resource PC is a virtual robot connected to Blue Prism server.

▶ Option D is incorrect because session manager lists all the session.

Question: 170

ANSWER: **B**

▶ Option A is incorrect because control room is used to monitor the robots and running sessions.

▶ Option B is correct because system manger is used to add external web services into Blue Prism environment.

▶ Option C is incorrect because process studio is used to create the processes.

▶ Option D is incorrect because application modeller is used to spy the elements of application.

Question: 171

ANSWER: **B**

▶ Option A is incorrect because processes and objects can be over written in a Blue Prism environment when release is imported.

▶ Option B is correct because processes and objects can be over written in a Blue Prism environment when release is imported.

▶ Option C is incorrect because it's not required to delete and create new processes and objects.

▶ Option D is incorrect cause the BP objects can't be deleted cause of release.

Question: 172

ANSWER: **C**

▶ Option A is incorrect because break points will not stop the process.

▶ Option B is incorrect because break points will not restart the process.

▶ Option C is correct because a process can be set to pause on a specific stage if necessary.

▶ Option D is incorrect because break points are not used to immediate stop the robot. Immediate stop command should be sent from control room.

Question: 173

ANSWER: **C**

▶ Option A is incorrect because the data item can be type number.

▶ Option B is incorrect because data items with name "Number" can't not be created.

▶ Option C is correct because there is a stage/data item existing with the name "Number".

▶ Option D is incorrect because stage or data item is present with same name on page main.

Question: 174

ANSWER: **A**

▶ Option A is correct because get table native action of read stage is used to read the entire table form the application. Gets all elements of a HTML table, as a collection.

▶ Option B is incorrect because it gets the current value (of a textbox, combobox, listview current row, checkbox, etc.).

▶ Option C is incorrect because it gets the description of the accessibility element.

▶ Option D is incorrect because it gets the name of the accessibility element.

Question: 175

ANSWER: **B**

▶ Option A is incorrect because process would not skip the execution of other pages.

▶ Option B is correct cuase that process executes entire flow ans pauses at read details atage.

▶ Option C is incorrect because process does not skip the execution of read details stage.

▶ Option D is incorrect because "read details" stage would not be removed by seleting "run to this stage".

Question: 176

ANSWER: **C**

▶ Option A is incorrect because internal collection object does not contain action to remove blank rows from collections.

▶ Option B is incorrect because work queue object only contains actions related to work queues.

▶ Option C is correct because utility-collection manipulation object has action called "remove blank rows" to remove blank rows from collections.

▶ Option D Is incorrect because utility-general object has action like sleep, process info, etc.

Question: 177

ANSWER: **D**

▶ Option A is incorrect because Blue Prism does not support nested exception blocks.

▶ Option B is incorrect because exception blocks without recovery and resume stages will have no effect on the execution of the process.

▶ Option C is incorrect because exceptions in block 1 are caught by get details recovery stage.

▶ Option D is correct because blocks should not overlap, and blocks cannot be nested (i.e. Blocks within Blocks).

Question: 178

ANSWER: **C**

▶ Option A is incorrect because resume stage does not catch the exception.

▶ Option B is incorrect because resume stage neither catches exception nor throws the exception. Resume stage is used to neutralize the exception.

▶ Option C is correct because exception block with our resume stage has no effect hence exception bubbles up to next level.

▶ Option D is incorrect because process does not terminate as the logic is not on main page.

Question: 179

ANSWER: **B**

▶ Option A is incorrect because process would not skip the execution of other pages.

▶ Option B is correct cuase that process executes entire flow ans pauses at read details atage.

▶ Option C is incorrect because process does not skip the execution of read details stage.

▶ Option D is incorrect because "read details" stage would not be removed by seleting "run to this stage".

Question: 180

ANSWER: **D**

▶ Option A, B and C are not correct because control room, system manger, process studio does not interact with target application.

▶ Option D is correct cause object studio has application modeller embedded in it. Object studio is used to create actions to navigate through the application using the elements that are spied using application modeller.

Question: 181

ANSWER: **A**

▶ Option A is correct because a) Get Item Data is used to retrieve the data of the case only for report generation. This action can´t lock the case even though used on pending cases. Get Item data action can retrieve the data of case despite of the its status. If robot need to work about a queue case, get next action should be used to have the case locked. b) Unlock item is used to unlock the queue items which were locked by get next item or Lock Item actions. The purpose of using unlock item action is to maintain the case in pending status so that another robot will pick up the case to work on it.

▶ Option B is incorrect because a queue item should be in locked status for marking it as completed. Blue Prism does not natively provide "lock" action in its work Queues object.

▶ Option C is incorrect because a) Update status action is used to update the status of the case at run time. Updating status would facilitate the user to know the status of queue Item in case of exceptions and for report generation at the end of the execution of the robot.

▶ Option D Is incorrect cause of incorrect options 2 and 4.

Question: 182

ANSWER: **C**

▶ Option A is incorrect because session variables are specific to the Robot. Changes in any session variables will be reflected only in the robot corresponding to that session.

▶ Option B is incorrect because the purpose of these variable is completely different and can't be interchanged.

▶ Option C is correct because the motive of using session variable is to control the execution of the robot. Robot can change the flow based on the current session variable value.

▶ Option D is incorrect because environment variables should be used to store any process or application information required to work the business process that may be subject to change either between environments (development/test/production) or over time.

Question: 183

ANSWER: **C**

▶ Option A is incorrect because robot does not go into infinite loop since recovery stage already has the exception in it. If robot executes resume stage before throwing another exception, Robot would go into infinite exception loop.

▶ Option B is incorrect because run time errors can't impact the start of the execution. Only complier errors that we see in errors section of process studio would prevent the start of the execution.

▶ Option C is correct because every recovery stage can hold only one exception. In above scenario if robot tries to execute recovery second time, Blue Prism throws the exception with the details of the exception stage.

▶ Option D is not correct because robot would never skip an action defined in its flow.

Question: 184

ANSWER: **A**

▶ Option A is correct cause action stage is present in both object studio and process studio. This stage is used to call actions from another object. In object studio, one can call actions from other objects.

▶ Option B is incorrect because wait stage is unique to the object studio. Wait stage is used to conditional wait for the element to be loaded on target application. Since process studio does not perform actions on target application directly, this action is not present in process studio.

▶ Option C is incorrect because code stage is only present in object studio. Using code stage once write code in C#, Visual basics and F#.

▶ Option D is incorrect cause the read stage is specific to the object studio. Read stage is used to read the values from elements of the target application. If Process needs to read value from a text box, in such case read can be used to read the value.

Question: 185

ANSWER: **B**

▶ Option A is incorrect because process can have exception logic implemented in it. The statement is incorrect that only objects can have Resume stages.

▶ Option B is correct because one process can have multiple resume stages depending on the logic of the exception handling. As per Blue Prism best practice guide, exception logic should be included in subpages, hence one process can have multiple number of resume stages.

▶ Option C is incorrect because of the explanation for option B. There is no limit to resume stages in a process.

▶ Option D is incorrect cause a process can have resume stage even it does not have exception block that means any exception occurs in process would be caught by that resume stage.

Question: 186

ANSWER: D

▶ Option A is not correct because wait stage does not wait to start looking for the element.

▶ Option B is incorrect because though wait stage does start looking for element immediately, code doesn't wait for 5 secs to execute navigate stage to click the button.

▶ Option C is incorrect because exception would not be thrown if element is found in 5 sec. if element is found code will execute the following navigate stage.

▶ Option D is correct as wait stage does start looking for immediately for 5 seconds and will throw system exception if element is not found in 5 secs.

Question: 187

ANSWER: C

▶ Option A is incorrect that as per Blue Prism development best practices. If credentials are saved in data item, process code should be changed every time user changes the password.

▶ Option B is incorrect because Session variables are data items that can be modified at run time from control room. Any configuration that may need changing while a process session is running can be exposed as a Session variable.

▶ Option C is correct because blue prism provides a secure way of storing sensitive data using inbuilt module called credential manager.

▶ Option D is incorrect because environment variables should be used to store any process or application information required to work the business process that may be subject to change either between environments or over time.

Question: 188

ANSWER: **A**

▶ Option A is correct because global send Key events method is used to send the special events or keys to the target application. The events should be enclosed in curly braces. The modifiers "<" and ">" change the following letter into a key-down or key-up operation (respectively). "<{CTRL}s>{CTRL}" simulates depressing the control key, pressing "s" and releasing the control key again.

▶ Option B is incorrect because though global send key event is used, the input value to function is syntactically incorrect.

▶ Option C is incorrect because global send key function sends input value to the target application. It does not support the key up and key down operations.

▶ Option D is incorrect cause global send key function does not support the key up and key down operations.

Question: 189

ANSWER: **D**

Below is the role matrix of Blue Prism delivery road map.

Document	Created By
Initial Process Analysis	Blue Prism analyst or Blue Prism developer
Process Definition Document	Client SME and/or Blue Prism analyst
Functional Requirements Questionnaire	Client SME and/or Blue Prism analyst
Solution Design Document	Blue Prism developer
Operational Impact Document	Blue Prism analyst
Process Design Instruction	Blue Prism developer
Object Design Instruction	Blue Prism developer

▶ Option A is incorrect because Process definition document is created by Process Analyst.

▶ Option B is incorrect because Operational Impact Document is created by Process Analyst.

▶ Option C is incorrect because Functional Requirements Questionnaire (FRQ) and Operational Impact Document (OID) are created by Process Analyst.

▶ Option D is correct because Process Design Instruction (PDI) and Object Design Instruction (ODI) should be created by Blue Prism Developer.

Question: 190

ANSWER: D

▶ Option A is incorrect cause of wrong syntax. Tag filter does not support OR operator.

▶ Option B is incorrect because tag filter parameter "1;4" would fetch the case items that are tagged 1 and 4. Below is the sample case.

Item Key	Priority	Status	Tags
••• test	0		1;4

▶ Option C is incorrect cause of incorrect syntax.

▶ Option D is correct because each term in tag filter can be separated by a semi-colon and they are all applied to the search (ie. they are AND'ed terms not OR'ed terms). Hence to get the case which are tagged as 1 or 4, tag filter should be applied to exclude cases which are tagged 2 and 3.

Appendix 4

PROFESSIONAL DEVELOPER ANSWERS

Question: 1

ANSWER: **A**

- ▶ Option A is correct because custom filters of the queue view should be separated by comma, and Option A states the range between 01-01-2018 and 01-12-2018.

- ▶ Option B is incorrect because filter specifies that cases that are not created between 01-01-2018 and 01-12-2018.

- ▶ Option C is incorrect cause of the syntactical error. Comma should be used in custom filters of queue view.

- ▶ Option D is incorrect cause of the syntactical error. Comma should be used in custom filters of queue view.

Question: 2

ANSWER: **D**

All the application modes of Blue Prism can be used to identify the browser applications. Blue Prism object of browser application can be comprised of elements of various modes.

Browser main window is identified using win32 or AA and browser application's elements can be identified by any of the modes.

Question: 3

OPTIONS: **A**

▶ Option A is correct because Blue Prism uses the grid tool to identify rectangular areas of the screen. Application modeller does this by superimposing a grid onto the application to make the rows and columns of the screen visible. One unit of the grid represents one-character space on the screen.

▶ Option B is incorrect because JAB (Java access bridge) is used to connect to java applications.

▶ Option C is incorrect because AA (active accessibility) is used to interact with some windows type complex applications.

▶ Option D is incorrect because Spy++ has a toolbar and hyperlinks to help you work faster. It also provides a Refresh command to update the active view, a window finder tool to make spying easier.

Question: 4

ANSWER: **A**

▶ Option A is correct because one should be followed below steps to activate JAB in windows machines 7.

1. Go to Start > Control Panel > Ease of Access > Ease of Access Center. Alternatively, press Windows logo key+u to access the Ease of Access Center
2. Select Use the computer without a display
3. In the section Other programs installed, select the check box Enable Java Access Bridge (you may have to scroll down)

▶ Hence options B, C and C are incorrect.

Question: 5

ANSWER: **A**

▶ Option A is correct because having multiple objects within the object layer provides a more efficient and scalable design because:

● More developers can work concurrently

- A running process consumes only the actions it requires

- Application modeller is smaller and less prone to latent error

- Whenever a change is made within the object layer the effect on and risk to the process layer is minimised

▶ Option B is incorrect because multiple objects within the object layer make the process consume only the actions it requires resulting process running faster.

▶ Option C is incorrect because one object per application is not efficient cause of difficulties in maintainability and scalability.

▶ Option D is incorrect because multiple objects in object layer does not consume more memory while running the process.

Question: 6

ANSWER: **A**

▶ Option A is correct because Blue Prism's windows application native connector is used to interact with adobe application on windows machine. Adobe acrobat reader is a windows application.

▶ Option B is incorrect because Java application connector can't be used to connect to the adobe application.

▶ Option C is incorrect because Mainframe application connector can't be used to connect to the adobe application.

▶ Option D is incorrect because Database application connector is not available in Blue Prism application modeller.

Question: 7

ANSWER: **A**

▶ Option A is correct cause of right syntax.

▶ Option B, C and D are syntactically wrong.

Question:8

ANSWER: **A**

▶ Option A is correct because Blue Prism does not provide native support for Blowfish encryption algorithm.

▶ Option B is incorrect because AES-256 AESCryptoService is a native supported algorithm by Blue Prism.

▶ Option C is incorrect because AES-256 RijndaelManaged is a native supported algorithm by blue prism.

▶ Option D is incorrect because 3DES is a native supported algorithm by blue prism.

Question: 9

ANSWER: **B**

▶ Option A is not correct because control room is used to monitoring the daily execution, queue status and schedules.

▶ Option B is correct because the screen capture feature must be enabled in the system settings for the checkbox to take any effect. Option C is incorrect because Process studio is used to create the process containing business logic and business rules.

▶ Option D is incorrect because object studio is used to spy the elements of the target application and to create actions to interact with the application.

Question: 10

ANSWER: **C**

▶ Option A is incorrect because business exception are exceptions raised by unknow data from input sources.

▶ Option B is incorrect because system exceptions are caused by target system's unresponsiveness.

▶ Option C is correct because Blue Prism throws internal exception when failed to identify elements.

▶ Option D is incorrect because invalid element exception type does not exist.

Question:11

ANSWER: C

▶ Option A is incorrect because stopped status will be shown when user stops the session from control room.

▶ Option B is incorrect cause the immediately stopped status is not available in Blue Prism.

▶ Option C is correct because terminated status is shown in control room when process is stopped.

▶ Option D is incorrect because exception stopped is not available in Blue Prism.

Question: 12

ANSWER: A

▶ Option A is correct because combination of tags in the Tag Filter parameter is used to get filter the work queue, separated by semi-colons. By setting the Tag Filter to be "+Work Type5; +Customer Type10; -branch type 10" the next item with the "Work Type5" and "Customer Type10" tags and without a "branch type 10" tag will be returned.

▶ Option B is incorrect because tag filter parameter "Work Type5; Customer Type10; branch type10" would fetch the case items that are tagged "Work Type5; Customer Type10; branch type10". IN this case get next item action would not return any work queue case.

▶ Option C is incorrect cause of incorrect syntax.

▶ Option D is incorrect because the configuration fetches the cases that which are not tagged as worktype5 and customer type 10 and which are tagged as branch type 10.

Question: 13

ANSWER: **A**

▶ Option A is correct because Tag searches support two wildcards. An asterisk character is used to search for 'any other characters', and a question mark character is used to search for 'any single character'. For example, "+Type: Account*" will return items which have a tag beginning " Type: Account " and exclude any items which aren't assigned such a tag. A search for "Priority?" will return any items which have a tag beginning 'Priority ' followed by a single character.

▶ Option B is incorrect because "?" is used for single characters and *is used for any other characters.

▶ Option C is incorrect because tag is used only for filtering the work queue.

▶ Option D is incorrect since option A is correct.

Question: 14

ANSWER: **A**

When first created on a queue, an item has a workflow status of Pending. When selected to be worked by a process, it is Locked, following which the process can elect to set the workflow status of the item to Completed (to indicate that the item has been processed successfully), Exceptioned (to indicate that the item has failed in some way while attempting to process it) or Deferred (to defer processing of the item until a later date).

▶ Hence the correct option is A.

Question: 15

ANSWER: **C**

▶ Option A is incorrect because \ escaping character is not valid in Blue Prism.

▶ Option B is incorrect because / escaping character is not valid in Blue Prism.

▶ Option C is correct because to search for literal asterisks, they can be escaped by entering them in the search twice.

▶ Option D is incorrect "+*" return the cases which are tagged as +*.

Question: 16

ANSWER: **A**

▶ Option A is correct because the status can be used as a way of recording what work has been done so far on a Work Queue item. Using update status action work queue status can be updated multiple times.

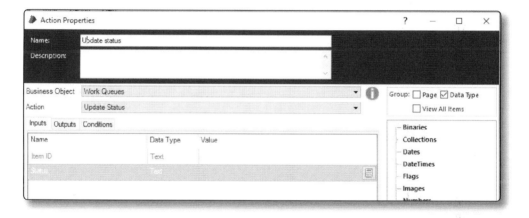

▶ Option B is incorrect because status can be set in the middle of the process as well.

▶ Option C is incorrect because work queue status cannot be deleted once its added. Status can only be updated.

▶ Option D is incorrect.

Question: 17

ANSWER: **D**

▶ Options A, B and C are incorrect because Blue Prism uses google testtract OCR engine for surface automation.

There are Blue Prism objects to use Google cloud vision, IBM Data Cap, Abbyy SDK services in automated processes.

Question: 18

ANSWER: **A**

▶ Option A is correct because work queue object set priority action can be used to update or set the priority of the work queue.

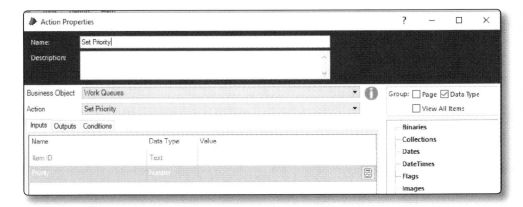

▶ Option B and option C are incorrect because update priority actions Is not available in work queue object.

▶ Option D is incorrect there exist an action to modify the priority.

Question: 19

ANSWER: **B**

By default, the order in which items are selected by Get Next Item is First-In-First-Out (FIFO), or in other words, the same order in which they were added to the queue. However, this order can be modified by setting up the priority of case while adding to queue.

▶ Hence the option is B.

Question: 20

ANSWER: **A**

Get Next Item selects items in order of lowest Priority number first, so an item with Priority set to 1 will be selected before an item with Priority set to 2.

▶ Hence the Option A is correct.

Question: 21

ANSWER: **B**

▶ Option A is not correct because control room is used to monitoring the daily execution, queue status and schedules.

▶ Option B is correct cause to change the encryption scheme or disable encryption system manager module of Blue Prism is used. Then selecting drop down list to choose the encryption state of the queue.

▶ Option C is incorrect because process studio is used to create the process containing business logic and business rules.

▶ Option D is incorrect because object studio is used to spy the elements of the target application and to create actions to interact with the application.

Question: 22

ANSWER: **A**

- ▸ Option A is correct because system exceptions can be reworked as they are raised by errors in target system integration with blue Prism. These kinds of exception can be solved once the target system is restarted.

- ▸ Option B is incorrect because Business exception can be raised cause of unknown user input. This kind of cases should be reported to user to proceed manually.

- ▸ Option C is incorrect because invalid input exception is caused of new type of input. These exceptions should be reported to users.

- ▸ Option D is incorrect because system exceptions can be reworked after restarting the system.

Question: 23

ANSWER: **B**

- ▸ Option A is incorrect because diving the process' work between robot and running them on different machines costs licenses that are equal to the number of machines.

- ▸ Option B is correct because Using a single Work Queue and deferring the case item for a week make the developer consume one license and complete the total work of the process.

- ▸ Option C is incorrect because Blue Prism can automate the entire process without human intervention by using Multi-Part Processes – Deferring and Multiple Queues technique of work queue management.

- ▸ Option D is incorrect because Blue Prism can automate processes which are of multi part.

Question: 24

ANSWER: **B**

- ▸ Option A is incorrect because Blue Prism process cannot know take from the newly constructed queues dynamically.

▶ Option B is correct because by using the tag of work queue case, work cases can be filtered and worked differently.

▶ Option C is incorrect because different mail boxes and different robots costs many licenses and additional logic.

▶ Option D is incorrect because Blue Prism provides mechanism to automate this kind of processes.

Question: 25

ANSWER: C

▶ Option A is incorrect because navigate stage should be used to attach to the target application.

▶ Option B is incorrect because if Blue Prism identifies more than one element with same foot print, below exception will be thrown.

"Internal: more than one element found for footprint"

▶ Option C is correct because 'Target application could not be identified' conveys that it can't find the application to attach to. In most of the cases this exception occurs when application is not launch.

▶ Option D is incorrect because the exception is not Blue Prism internal exception.

Question: 26

ANSWER: D

▶ Option A is incorrect because multi-part processes methodology is used for multi processes which has time gap between two parts of the process.

▶ Option B is incorrect because Parent/Child Relationships is used where multiple Work Queue items must be linked to a single request.

▶ Option C is incorrect because work systems can be used to populate work queues.

▶ Option D is correct because manual creation is never a design methodology of work queue.

Question: 27

ANSWER: C

- ▶ Option A is incorrect because page fails with the exception.

- ▶ Option B is incorrect because there is no specific order to do attach and launch.

- ▶ Option C is correct because launching an application attaches the business object automatically. Once a business object has been attached to an application, any attempt to attach again will cause an exception.

- ▶ Option D is incorrect because launch stage does not throw exception.

Question: 28

ANSWER: D

Having multiple resumes / recover stages on a page is redundant. Any exception will be caught by first recover stage and will be follow its flow.

- ▶ Hence the correct option is D.

Question: 29

ANSWER: A

Having multiple resumes / recover stages on a page is redundant. Any exception will be caught by first recover stage and will be follow its flow.

- ▶ Hence the correct option is A.

Question: 30

ANSWER: D

- ▶ Option A, B and c are not correct because they all are internal exceptions.

- ▶ Option D is correct because validation exception can be thrown at the time of input validation. Validation depends on the process scope.

Question: 31

ANSWER: **A**

▶ Option A is correct because retry exception logic is implemented in subpages to avoid infinite loops or more retries than designed.

▶ Option B is incorrect because process decision should be designed at process level.

▶ Option C is incorrect because main page cannot be used to implement the retry logic in case of exceptions.

▶ Option D is incorrect because retry logic is implemented in subpages level.

Question: 32

ANSWER: **D**

▶ Option A is incorrect because action stage is used to call pages in business objects. If action stage has error, it would prevent the process from successful execution.

▶ Option B is incorrect because recover stage is used to catch the exception raised in exception block. if exception blocks are not used, recover stage catches the exception on the page.

▶ Option C is incorrect because resume stage is used to neutralize the exception raised on the page.

▶ Option D is correct because Exception Block is used to isolate the exception on a page.

Question: 33

ANSWER: **A**

▶ Option A is correct because this decision ensures the flow only retries if the Retry Count has not been reached and if the exception type is either a System Exception or an Internal Exception.

▶ Option B is incorrect because this decision ensures the flow only retries if the Retry Count greater than the limit and if the exception type is either a System Exception or an Internal Exception.

▶ Option C is incorrect because this decision ensures the flow only retries if the Retry Count has not been reached and if the exception type is not a System Exception or exception type is an Internal Exception.

▶ Option D is incorrect because this decision ensures the flow only retries if the Retry Count has not been reached and if the exception type is a System Exception or exception type is not an Internal Exception.

Question: 34

ANSWER: C

▶ Option A is incorrect because Resume can be connected to end stage.

▶ Option B is incorrect because Anchor stage can be connected from start stage.

▶ Option C is correct because the page is missing recover stage and resume stage is implemented without recover stage. Process will be terminated in case of exceptions from action from the page.

▶ Option D is incorrect because resume stage is missing on the page.

Question: 35

ANSWER: C

▶ Option A is incorrect because recover2 stage has no effect on the page.

▶ Option B is incorrect because Exception block in recover mode cannot isolate the exception.

▶ Option C is correct because process gets terminated with divide by zero exception. Exceptions occurred in recovery mode cannot themselves be recovered.

▶ Option D is incorrect because arithmetic exception would be caught by recover1 stage.

Question: 36

ANSWER: **D**

▶ Option A is not correct because control room is used to monitoring the daily execution, queue status and schedules.

▶ Option B is incorrect because Process studio is used to create the process containing business logic and business rules.

▶ Option C is incorrect because Dash board is used to configure titles for statistical information of robots.

▶ Option D is correct cause to change the encryption scheme or disable encryption system manager module of Blue Prism is used.

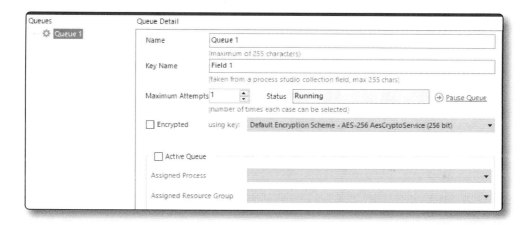

Question: 37

ANSWER: **B**

▶ Option A is incorrect because if an exception happens in recover mode, process gets terminated with second exception.

▶ Option B is correct because if end stage is executed while process in recover stage, stack imbalance error will happen.

▶ Option C is incorrect because process errors do not cause stack imbalance exception.

▶ Option D is incorrect cause missing recover stage causes process to be terminated.

Question: 38

ANSWER: **A**

▶ Option A is correct because arithmetic exception would be caught by recove1 stage.

▶ Option B is incorrect because divide by zero exception calculate stage terminates the process. Exceptions occurring during recovery mode cannot themselves be recovered.

▶ Option C and D are incorrect because recove1 stage catches arithmetic exception and recover stage2 has no effect on entire page.

Question: 39

ANSWER: **A**

▶ Option A is correct because Process follows the recover1 stage path as divide by zero stage is not linked in the process.

▶ Option B is incorrect because process does not get terminated cause of exception block overlapping.

▶ Option C is incorrect cause process start the execution despite of its errors.

▶ Option D is incorrect.

Question:40

ANSWER: **A**

If the properties of an unhandled exception stage are left blank, then it will generate an exception with no detail. This can have a knock-on effect on any subsequent exception handling.

▶ Hence the answer is A.

Question: 41

ANSWER: A

If the properties of an Exception stage are left blank, then it will generate an exception with no detail. This can have a knock-on effect on any subsequent exception handling or result in a queue item having no exception detail.

▶ Hence the answer is A.

Question: 42

ANSWER: A

▶ Option A is correct because having multiple objects within the object layer provides a more efficient and scalable design because more developers can work concurrently.

▶ Option B is incorrect using shifts to access the process is very inefficient way resource management.

▶ Option C is incorrect that dividing the process adds to the integration problems.

▶ Option D is incorrect because sharing user id is not recommended way of developing as per blue prism design structure.

Question: 43

ANSWER: A

▶ Option A is correct because one business object for every screen can be reutilized in various business processes. And whenever a change is made within the object layer the effect on and risk to the process layer is very minimised.

▶ Option B is incorrect because business object of the task can't be reutilized even another process uses same application page.

▶ Option C is incorrect because whenever a change is made within the object layer the effect on and risk to the process layer is very huge.

▶ Option D is incorrect because one business object for every screen of the application is recommended way of design.

Question: 44

ANSWER: **C**

▶ Option A is incorrect because wait stage should be implemented in all the actions which are interacting with the application.

▶ Option B is incorrect because action stage is used to call pages from another business object. Page stage is used to call pages from same business object.

▶ Option C is correct because business decisions should not happen in the object. Maintenance and change management will be difficult if logic is implemented in Business objects.

▶ Option D is incorrect because the mentioned page has business logic implemented in it.

Question: 45

ANSWER: **C**

"Request stop" sets the session variable "StopRequested" to true. To stop correctly, the worker process must check the IsStopRequested () function regularly, cleaning up its environment and exiting the process when the function indicates that a stop has been requested.

"Immediate stop" like killing the process. Immediate stop ends the execution leaving the current queue case as exception.

▶ Hence the correct answer is C.

Question: 46

ANSWER: **D**

Tags are individual text labels which can be assigned to items. They provide a means of grouping items together and can be used to filter items in the business object or in the contents list. Blue prism tags are semicolon separated values. New tags are appended to the list of existing tags.

Hence there is no limit on the number of tags of the work queue case

Question: 47

ANSWER: **D**

▶ Option A is not correct because control room is used to monitoring the daily execution, queue status and schedules.

▶ Option B is incorrect because Process studio is used to create the process containing business logic and business rules.

▶ Option C is incorrect because Dash board is used to configure titles for statistical information of Robots.

▶ Option D is correct cause to expose the processes or objects as web services system manager module of Blue Prism is used.

Question: 48

ANSWER: **A**

The web services that are exposed from Blue Prism can be confirmed by using the following URL which also provides the address of the WSDL.

http://[machinename]:[Blue Prism resource port]/ws/

In this example the machine name is resource001 and the default port of 8181 is in use:

http://resource001:8181/ws/

▶ Hence the correct option is A.

Question: 49

ANSWER: **A**

▶ Option A is correct that to expose a process as a web service, it must be published, and its name must contain only alphanumeric characters - i.e. no punctuation or space characters.

▶ Option B is incorrect because code stage is often useful for interfacing with a COM object in a Microsoft Windows environment. It's not mandatory to use code stage to expose as web service.

▶ Option C is incorrect because no configuration is required to expose the process or object as web service.

▶ Option D is incorrect because there is naming convention to expose blue prism objects as web services.

Question: 50

ANSWER: **B**

Once the services are added to Blue Prism in system manager, such services will be visible as business objects from Process Studio and can be called using an action stage.

▶ Hence the correct answer is B.

Question: 51

ANSWER: **A**

▶ Option A is correct because web services can also be registered via the commandline automate switch , using the /regwebservice command.

/addwerbservice, /esposewebservice, /modwebservice those commands are not available in Blue prism.

Question: 52

ANSWER: **A**

▶ Option A is correct because WSDL - Web Service Description Language. A WSDL document describes the capabilities provided by a web service, including what information is expected and what information will be returned.

Question: 53

ANSWER: **A**

▶ Option A is correct because flag data type of the blue prism is equivalent to the Boolean type of the .NET. Below table represents the type equivalence.

Blue Prism	.NET
date	Date
Time	Date time
Flag	Boolean
Number	Decimal
Text	String
time	Time
Time span	Duration

Question: 54

ANSWER: **D**

Blue Prism supports IP based authentication, certificate-based authentication and username and password as part of the HTTP header but does not support WS-Security authentication.

▶ Hence the answer is D.

Question:55

ANSWER: **A**

- ▶ Option A is correct because a code stage is often useful for interfacing with a COM object in a Microsoft windows environment.

- ▶ Option B is incorrect because action stage is used to call the pages of business object.

- ▶ Option C is incorrect because page stage is used to call another page of same business object.

- ▶ Option D is incorrect because Sub process stage is used to call another process.

Question: 56

ANSWER: **B**

When consuming web services, complex types (arrays, lists) they will be mapped into Collections within Blue Prism.

Numbers are used to map the int, float, decimal, etc.

String are used to map the string data types.

List data type is not available in Blue Prism.

- ▶ Hence Option B is the correct answer.

Question: 57

ANSWER: **C**

Each request to an exposed Process will require a new session to be created resulting in consumption of the license. If three processes are being consumed at a time, Blue Prism needs three separate licenses to create three concurrent sessions.

Question:58

ANSWER: **C**

Blue Prism will manage the assignment of requests to a session automatically for processing requests to exposed Business Objects where the connection is set to auto-initialization. only one session is created per resource pc to consume one object web services. As three objects with back ground run mode are exposed as services, three sessions will be created in the same resource PC to connect them simultaneously.

▶ Correct option is C.

Question: 59

ANSWER: C

Blue Prism will manage the assignment of requests to a session automatically for processing requests to exposed Business Objects where the connection is set to auto-initialization. Since the run mode of business objects is set to exclusive, 3 resource PCs will be required to connect to three business objects simultaneously.

Question: 60

ANSWER: B

Blue Prism will manage the assignment of requests to a session automatically for processing requests to exposed Business Objects where the connection is set to auto-initialization, hence only one session is created per resource pc to consume object services.

▶ Correct option is B

Question: 61

ANSWER: C

Blue Prism will manage the assignment of requests to a session automatically for processing requests to exposed Business Objects where the connection is set to auto-initialization. only one session is created per resource pc to consume one object web services. As three objects with Exclusive run mode are exposed as services, three sessions will be created in the same resource PC to connect them simultaneously consuming three licenses.

▶ Correct option is C.

Question: 62

ANSWER: B

Each caller will programmatically manage the session creation when manual-initialization is used. Normally caller would choose to create a session to handle multiple calls. At least one session is required to connect to the service.

▶ Hence the correct option is B.

Question: 63

ANSWER: C

There are two initialization methods to connect to business object which is exposed as webservice. They are

1. Manual-initialization - Each caller will programmatically manage the session creation resulting in that a single session can handle multiple requests

2. Auto-initialization - Blue Prism will manage the assignment of requests to a session for processing requests to exposed Business Objects where the connection is set to use auto-initialization.

Question: 64

ANSWER: C

Refer the description of the run modes

Run Mode

○ Foreground   If this object should never have more than one instance running at the same time on the same resource, set to Foreground. This business object can run at the same time as other background business objects.

○ Background   If this object is designed to support multiple instances running at the same time on the same resource, set to Background. This business object can run at the same time as a foreground business object or other background business objects.

◉ Exclusive   If this object should never be run at the same time as any other object, and requires exclusive access to the desktop, set to Exclusive. This business object can not run at the same time as any other business object.

▶ Option A is incorrect because two fore ground sessions can't run in a single machine. Foreground session can have back ground session running along with them.

▶ Option B is incorrect because two exclusive sessions can't run in a single machine. Exclusive session can't have neither back ground or fore ground session along with it.

▶ Option C is correct because Back ground run mode is used to create various background sessions in machines.

▶ Option D is incorrect because back ground run mode is used to have multiple sessions.

Question: 65

ANSWER: D

▶ Option A is incorrect because current active session is present for the execution of Process A (Foreground).

Machine 1 attempts to create a session for the first web service request however as it is not possible to create a Foreground session when Exclusive session is ready present. The request is rejected with a message indicating that the Runtime Resource is busy.

▶ Hence the correct answer is D.

Question: 66

ANSWER: D

▶ Option A is incorrect because current active session is present for the execution of Process A (Foreground).

Machine 1 attempts to create a session for the first web service request however as it is not possible to create a Foreground session when one of the same types is ready present. The request is rejected with a message indicating that the Runtime Resource is busy.

▶ Hence the correct answer is D.

Question: 67

ANSWER: **A**

Auto-Generate Code can be created using wsdl.exe or wsewsdl3.exe. these tools normally are installed with visual studio. Below is the syntax of using wsdl.exe

WSDL.exe

VB.NET
wsdl.exe /language:VB /out:"%TEMP%" http://example.com/wsService?wsdl l

C#
wsdl.exe /language:CS /out:"%TEMP%" http://example.com/wsService?wsdl

WSewsdl3.exe

VB.NET
Wsewsdl3.exe /language:VB /type:webClient /out:"%TEMP%" http://example.com/wsService?wsdl

C#
Wsewsdl3.exe /language:CS /type:webClient /out:"%TEMP%" http://example.com/wsService?wsdl

▶ Correct answer is A.

Question: 68

ANSWER: **A**

Unlike Business Objects, processes run once for each instance, only have one entry point and there are no explicit initialization or clean-up actions required.

▶ Correct answer is A.

Question: 69

ANSWER: **A**

Blue Prism web services are secured using HTTP authentication. Blue Prism user account is configured for each third-party provider that will be consuming exposed Blue Prism web services. The credentials for these users can then be used as part of the HTTP header authentication process.

▶ Correct answer is A.

Question: 70

ANSWER: **A**

The external web services will be added to Blue Prism environment from system manager module. Once listed, such services will be visible as business objects from Process Studio and may be called using an action stage.

Hence action stage is used to call the methods of external webservices.

Question: 71

ANSWER: **C**

▶ Option A is incorrect because Blue Prism attaches to the main parent process of the internet explorer.

▶ Option B is incorrect because Blue Prism attaches to the first tab of the internet explorer.

▶ Option C is correct because Blue Prism attaches to second tab of internet explorer as child index tab is 2.

▶ Option D is incorrect because error will be thrown while identifying "iexplorer.exe" process. Normally .exe does not have to be appended while specifying process name.

Question: 72

ANSWER: **C**

Internet Explorer sessions will run in separate Windows processes which are spawned from a primary IE process. Each session is given a unique index based on the order in which the process for that session is created. The main parent process is given the index of 0, whereas the first tab of the process is given the Child Index of 1. The Child Index parameter is specified in the attach action of a navigate stage.

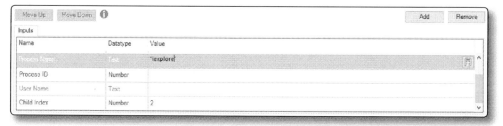

▶ Hence the correct answer is C.

Question: 73

ANSWER: **A**

▶ Option A is correct because get table native action of read stage is used to read the entire table form the application. Gets all elements of a HTML table, as a collection.

▶ Option B is incorrect because Gets the current value (of a textbox, combobox, listview current row, checkbox, etc).

▶ Option C is incorrect because Gets the description of the Accessibility element.

▶ Option D is incorrect because Gets the name of the Accessibility element.

Question: 74

ANSWER: **A**

In computing, Dynamic Data Exchange (DDE) is a method of interprocess communication under Microsoft Windows or OS/2. It allows one program to subscribe to items made available by another program, for example a cell in a Microsoft Excel spreadsheet, and be notified whenever that item changes. DDE was partially superseded by Object Linking and Embedding (OLE), but remains used for simple inter process communication tasks.

To create a DDE Element, right-click an existing element in the Application Modeller tree, and choose "Insert new DDE Element". You will then have to populate the three attributes according to your target application's definitions for the item of interest.

▶ Hence the correct answer is A.

Question: 75

ANSWER: **A**

▶ Option A is correct because Document Loaded checks if the current document has loaded. As the action is to perform on correct page, Document load checks if page is fully loaded.

▶ Option B is incorrect because Parent document checks the element exists and that the entire page and all its child frames are fully loaded.

▶ Option C is incorrect because check page exist does not exist.

▶ Option D is incorrect because Check Exists simply checks that the specified element exists on the page, regardless of if any other elements exist.

Question: 76

ANSWER: B

▶ Option A is incorrect because Document Loaded checks if the current document has loaded. As the action is to perform on correct page, Document load checks if page is fully loaded.

▶ Option B is correct because Parent document checks the element exists and that the entire page and all its child frames are fully loaded.

▶ Option C is incorrect because check page exist does not exist.

▶ Option D is incorrect because Check Exists simply checks that the specified element exists on the page, regardless of if any other elements exist.

Question: 77

ANSWER: C

▶ Option A, B and D are incorrect because HTML mode has parent URL, Path and Class name attributes.

▶ Option C is correct because Style is win32 attribute.

Question: 78

ANSWER: A

Silverlight applications have a property which allows them to be displayed as a windowless plug-in, which is usually set to true. To automate Silverlight applications the windowless property needs to be set to false. One way this can be achieved is by injecting some JavaScript into the browser to change the property to false and then invoking that JavaScript, which will allow the browser to expose the Active Accessibility properties of the elements to the blue prism.

▶ Correct answer is A.

Question: 79

ANSWER: **B**

▶ Option A is incorrect because insert JavaScript Fragment is used to insert small java script functions into web application.

▶ Option B is correct because It can be convenient to call a JavaScript function which is defined in the HTML of the web page you are interfacing with yourself. You can do this by using the Invoke JavaScript Function action.

▶ Option C and D are incorrect because call JavaScript and Execute JavaScript actions are not available in Blue Prism.

Question: 80

ANSWER: **D**

Any ActiveX components within target browser application that need to be automated, Surface Automation techniques should be used.

Question: 81

ANSWER: **A**

Session identifier needs to be mentioned when starting or attaching to a mainframe session. This can be hardcoded in Application Modeller or set dynamically via parameters on the Launch and Attach stages.

▶ Hence correct answer is A.

Question: 82

ANSWER: **C**

Sometimes launching a mainframe app causes an error message: "Unable to load DLL 'HLLAPI32.DLL': The specified module could not be found".

This is due to the mainframe installation directory is not added to the Windows PATH environment variable.

Question: 83

ANSWER: **A**

The send keys mainframe function takes a sequence of letters and control codes. To send the keys 'u' 's' 'e' 'r' 'ENTER' then the following sequence is used: "user{enter}".

Question: 84

ANSWER: **B**

Business Objects that model 32-bit Java applications must be set to "embedded" mode. There should be java 32-bit version installed on resource PC to integrate with java application with embedded application mode.

Question: 85

ANSWER: **C**

Business Objects that model 64-bit Java applications must be set to "External 64-bit" mode.

▶ Correct answer is C.

Question: 86

ANSWER: **A**

▶ Option A is correct because the application navigator will scan the Application Model tree for all the elements it can find. When an element is selected in the tree it will be highlighted within the application for confirmation and its attributes will be displayed.

▶ Option B is incorrect because DDE elements are used to inter process communication under windows environment.

▶ Option C is incorrect because HTC components option is used when business object is interacting with application which has HTC modules.

HTML Components (HTCs) are a legacy technology[1] used to implement components in script as Dynamic HTML (DHTML) "behaviors"[2] in the Microsoft Internet Explorer web browser. Such files typically use an .htc extension and the "text/x-component" MIME type.

▶ Option D is incorrect because diagnostics is used to trouble shooting problems.

Question: 87

ANSWER: **B**

▶ Option A is incorrect because Descendtree causes Blue Prism to search the entire Application Model Tree for elements within the target Java application. If this option is not set, Blue Prism will only directly retrieve a list of visible Java elements for each visible window in the target application.

▶ Option B is correct because ignorenotshowing will tell Blue Prism to ignore elements in the Application Model Tree which are below elements which are reported to be not showing.

▶ Option C is incorrect because ancestor count is application modeller attribute, it's not a value provided by blue prism support.

▶ Option D is incorrect because NotShowing option is not available.

Question: 88

ANSWER: **A**

▶ Option A is correct because Descendtree causes Blue Prism to search the entire Application Model Tree for elements within the target Java application. If this option is not set, Blue Prism will only directly retrieve a list of visible Java elements for each visible window in the target application.

▶ Option B is incorrect because ignorenotshowing will tell Blue Prism to ignore elements in the Application Model Tree which are below elements which are reported to be not showing.

▶ Option C is incorrect because ancestor count is application modeller attribute, it's not a value provided by blue prism support.

▶ Option D is incorrect because NotShowing option is not available.

Question: 89

ANSWER: **A**

Optical character recognition (also optical character reader, OCR) is the mechanical or electronic conversion of images of typed, handwritten or printed text into machine-encoded text, whether from a scanned document, a photo of a document, a scene-photo.

OCR technique should be used to extract data from scanned images from PDF documents.

Question: 90

ANSWER: **C**

Adobe Acrobat is a family of application software and Web services developed by Adobe Inc. to view, create, manipulate, print and manage files in Portable Document Format.

Adobe acrobat PDF reader should be used to interface with PDF documents.

Question: 91

ANSWER: **A**

For these images only the ' Reading Text with OCR' technique can be used to extract data. OCR will only work if the image is of a high enough quality, 300dpi is recommended as a minimum. The OCR engine used by Blue Prism can extract data from PDF images to certain confidence level.

Question: 92

ANSWER: **A**

There must not be a requirement to press CTRL + ALT + DEL prior to the user name and password fields being presented.

[Local Security Policy: Interactive Login: Do not require CTRL + ALT + DEL: Enabled]

Ctrl+ALT+Del should be disabled for login agent to work in resource PC.

▶ Correct answer is A.

Question: 93

ANSWER: **A**

Security→ Manage Credential permission should be given to a user to access the credentials tab in system manager.

▸ Hence correct answer is A.

Question: 94

ANSWER: **C**

The Credentials Management functionality provides a secure repository for sensitive information used to access target applications. Credentials are stored in the Blue Prism database but are encrypted in such a way that only those who are authorized can retrieve them. other properties can also be saved in Credential manager as shown below.

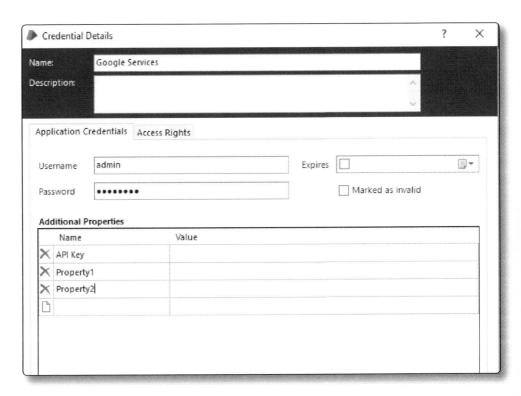

Question: 95

ANSWER: **D**

▶ Options A, B and C are incorrect because those actions are not available in credential business object.

▶ Option D is correct because get property should be used to get the values of credential properties. Credential Name and Property Name should be pass as input parameters to the action.

Question: 96

ANSWER: **B**

▶ Option A is not correct because control room is used to monitoring the daily execution, queue status and schedules.

▶ Option B is correct because system manager module is used to create custom calendar to be used in blue prism processes.

▶ Option C is incorrect because process studio is used to create the process containing business logic and business rules.

▶ Option D is incorrect because object studio is used to spy the elements of the target application and to create actions to interact with the application.

Question: 97

ANSWER: **A**

FQDN (fully qualified domain name) should be used when various domain machines are configured in Blue Prism.

Hence all resource PCs should be registered using either short name or FQDN, but communication should happen using FQDN.

Question: 98

ANSWER: **D**

▶ Option A is incorrect because Active Accessibility mode should be used with application which exposes its elements using Microsoft active accessibility.

▶ Option B is incorrect because win32 mode is used to spy the windows applications.

▶ Option C is incorrect because HTML mode is used to spy the web applications.

▶ Option D is correct because region mode is used to spy the images or thin client applications.

Question: 99

ANSWER: **C**

▶ Option A is incorrect because java automation techniques should be used to automate java applications.

▶ Option B is incorrect because Browser automation is used to automate browser applications.

▶ Option C is correct because surface automation should be used to automate applications that are hosted in Citrix.

▶ Option D is incorrect because Citrix automation is not valid automation technique of Blue Prism.

Question: 100

ANSWER: D

▶ Option A, B and C are incorrect because read text, read image, recognise text are present as functions in reader stage of region elements.

▶ Option D is correct because Recognise images data function is not available in blue prism.

Question: 101

ANSWER: B

▶ Option B is correct because Utility- Image Manipulation is used in surface automation.

Question: 102

ANSWER: A

▶ Option A is correct because Read Text with OCR reads text using OCR from a rectangular area on a window.

▶ Option B is incorrect because Read Text reads text discovered using invasive techniques within a rectangular area of a window.

▶ Option C and D are not available methods in Blue Prism.

Question: 103

ANSWER: **B**

> ▶ Option A is incorrect because Read Text with OCR reads text using OCR from a rectangular area on a window.

> ▶ Option B is correct because Read Text reads text discovered using invasive techniques within a rectangular area of a window.

> ▶ Option C and D are not available methods in Blue Prism.

Question: 104

ANSWER: **A**

To add support for another language, appropriate files should be downloaded and copied to the Tesseract\tessdata folder in Blue prism installation directory.

Question: 105

ANSWER: **A**

To maximise the effectiveness of the recognition a minimum of 300 dots-per-inch (dpi) is required.

> ▶ Hence the correct answer is A.

Printed in Great Britain
by Amazon